Martingale®
& COMPANY

Skirts

ReSew

turn thrift-store finds into fabulous designs

Jenny Wilding Cardon

Martingale®
& C O M P A N Y

CREDITS

President & CEO: Tom Wierzbicki

Editor in Chief: Mary V. Green

Managing Editor: Tina Cook

Developmental Editor: Karen Costello Soltys

Technical Editor: Ellen Pahl

Copy Editor: Candie Frankel

Design Director: Stan Green

Production Manager: Regina Girard

Illustrator: Jenny Wilding Cardon

Cover & Text Designer: Shelly Garrison

Photographer: Brent Kane

Author photographs on pages 8, 9, and back flap by JuanitaB Photography.

MISSION STATEMENT

Dedicated to providing quality products and service to inspire creativity.

ReSew: Turn Thrift-Store Finds into Fabulous Designs
© 2011 by Jenny Wilding Cardon

Martingale & Company
19021 120th Ave. NE, Suite 102
Bothell, WA 98011-9511 USA
www.martingale-pub.com

Printed in China
16 15 14 13 12 11   8 7 6 5 4 3 2 1

Library of Congress Cataloging-in-Publication Data is available upon request.

ISBN: 978-1-60468-027-0

DEDICATION

For Brett, Jack, and Charlie—my three best boys, my three biggest supporters, my three life loves.

ACKNOWLEDGMENTS

Thank you to Mary Green and Karen Soltys at Martingale & Company—for believing I could write this book, and then for actually *letting* me write this book. And a special thank-you to Tina Cook for bringing up the whole crazy idea. I would have never thought to tackle this project at this time in my life. But the help of all of the talented, warmhearted people at this publishing house made it possible. Thanks to all of you, again.

Thank you to my friend and mother-in-law, Mary Ann Cardon, and my dear sister, Melainie Garcia, for spending time with our boys one day a week, three to four hours a visit, so I could meet my deadline (I came really close!). I know you both love our boys so much. They love you both so much, too.

Thank you to Mary Ann Cardon, Melainie Garcia, and Jeralyn Miller, who let me borrow their beautiful handmade jewelry to dress up my designs.

Thank you to my friend, Melissa Crumley, who showed me by example that what I am doing with my life—staying home with our boys, thrifting, sewing, frugaling, cooking, preserving, creating a soft place to fall, keeping up with laundry, kissing boo-boos, reading stories, teaching, learning, dancing, laughing—is an admirable, challenging, joyful art.

what's INSIDE

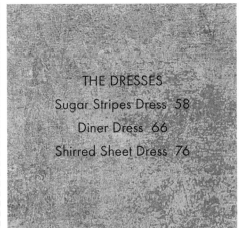

the ReSew revolution

I *am* Molly Ringwald in *Pretty in Pink*.
And you can be, too.

My introduction to thrifting came at a transitional time in my life—during my college years. I had just moved into an apartment all my own. Hooray! No more dorm rooms! No more roommates! No more sharing kitchens, bathrooms, and bedrooms!

And no more sharing the rent.

Not to mention, no more kitchen table, no more desk, no more lamps, no more chairs, no more couch. And no money to spare. I needed a quick way to furnish my new third-floor apartment at a bargain-basement price.

So I decided to try my luck at the local thrift store. The first item on my long list of must-haves? A couch.

Within minutes of entering the thrift store, I had found a jackpot of a couch. It was clean, it was comfortable, and it was covered in colorful bursts of poppies. And it was *big*. Big enough to seat four or five people, at least. I loved it! I bought the couch for a very reasonable price with a promise to the cashier that I would return the next day to take it home.

My long-time friend, Matt, helped me transport my new-to-me couch home. We arrived at my apartment and hauled the couch to the bottom of the winding outdoor staircase that led to my apartment door. Hands shading our eyes from the late-summer sun, we squinted up the staircase and sighed. A big couch. A big job.

We spent half an hour lifting, lowering, angling, tilting, and turning that couch to get it to the top of those three flights of stairs. But we did it. Sweaty and relieved, I pushed my shiny new key into the lock and opened my front door. And after another half an hour of lifting, lowering, angling, tilting, and turning that couch, we came to a conclusion: that gargantuan, poppy-covered couch would not fit through my front door. Not even a little bit. (Sorry, Matt. I'm still very sorry.)

That first introduction to thrifting—ill fated as it turned out to be—didn't dishearten me. In fact, that visit to the thrift store enchanted me. I felt like a rebellion had fired up in me. A personal revolution. And later, as I thrifted more often, a political revolution. Over time, I realized that thrift-store shopping was not just a way to be cost conscious (although striving to be cleverly, ingeniously, and artfully frugal is one of my passions). It was my opportunity to save money; to spend locally; to stretch my creativity (with my found treasures *and* my dollars); to help lighten a strain on the environment; and, mostly, to uncover the distinct and unique—and remake it, too—among the swell of mass-producing, big-box retailers that often promote the impersonal and uninspired. So, yeah, it's safe to say it. I was hooked.

The thrift-store experience marries my practical, utilitarian side with my creative, imaginative side. When I do my thrift-shop hops (weekly, at least), I'm not

stepping into spaces where anyone is trying to dictate what is hot, what is hip, and what is a "must-have" for me, my family, or our way of life. At the thrift store, no one cares about that. It's just me, walking in to discover what I like, what I need, what I want, what I can create. It's freeing. It's liberating. It's fun.

Are you feeling revolutionary yet?

There's a wonderful children's book—*Joseph Had a Little Overcoat*, by Simms Taback—that I read to my two sons often. Joseph had an overcoat, which over time became old and worn. He resewed his overcoat into a jacket; then a vest; then a tie; then a handkerchief; and finally a button. (He's even more frugal than I am.) And then Joseph lost the button.

You may think that's where the story ends. But it's precisely where the story begins. Because after Joseph loses the button, he realizes he still has something left of his overcoat. What he has is the story. So he writes the story he has about his overcoat and shares it with the world. And he wins the 1977 Caldecott Medal for the most distinguished picture book of the year. (Actually, that last part is not in the story. That's real life. The author won the medal. But I think Joseph should have won too.)

Now that I am, at this very moment, carefully packaging and organizing everything I've created to put on these pages, I see the connection between Joseph and me. I've recycled and resewn the best I know how. And now here's my story. In stitches. I hope you enjoy it.

Make everything,

Jenny

Whether your trips to the thrift store are centered on creativity, frugality, the environment, or just pure entertainment (of which there's lots to be had!), the projects in *ReSew* are fashioned to touch on them all. To keep the projects simple, I chose the most common thrift-store items: roomy T-shirts, men's dress pants, denim jeans, sweatshirts, sweaters, and linens—things that *you* can easily find, too. But here's the best thing of all: Even if you follow the project instructions to the letter, you're going to create something that's one of a kind. Heck, even if *I* follow my own instructions to the letter, I'm going to come up with something that's one of a kind. Again. What you choose as your foundation for re-creating a piece will be unique from the start; the one-of-a-kind results naturally follow. If I make 100 Knit-Knot T-shirts (page 24), I'll undoubtedly wind up with 100 originals, each with its own style and sass. Cool.

Thrifting is a bit of an art, but you also need a good mix of common sense and patience. Over my years of thrift-store shopping, I've come up with a few tips to help curb buyer's remorse. (Yes, you can get that at the thrift store, too.)

Keep an open mind. And open eyes. Looking for something particular during a thrift-store visit? Great—let the treasure hunt begin! But when you've found it—or even if you haven't—wander up and down each aisle before you make your way out. You simply never, *never* know what you might find. If you enter looking for a summer skirt and exit with a much wanted, like-new Belgian waffle maker, call your hunt triumphant.

Keep a list of things you'd like to find. My reference to a Belgian waffle maker wasn't pulled out of thin air. I really did want a Belgian waffle maker. I just didn't want to spend $50 to $70 on a new one. So I put it on the thrift-shop wish list I keep on the side of my fridge. After four months of taking my list with me on my weekly trips, I found exactly what I wanted. Like-new condition, plugged-in, fully tested. For $5. Triumphant! (Not to mention the years and years of yummy ahead.)

My list is a running list, and it can change from week to week. Sometimes I end up buying new instead.

Sometimes, a few weeks or a few months later, I realize I wrote down something that I don't really need or want anymore. There's a fine line to walk between keeping an open mind and keeping a list. A list can help keep your purchases in check.

Shop for the opposite season you're in. One of my favorite thrift stores sells T-shirts and tank tops at 50% off all winter long. I stock up; when I get home, I sit by the fire and dream about summer. People typically recycle their winter goods in spring and their summer goods in autumn. Keep your list updated to take advantage of those times.

Try it on. Spread it out. Find a problem? Do without. My number one rule for buying secondhand clothing? Try it on. Even if you are transforming a piece of clothing into something that won't be worn on your body, try it on. There's no better way to spot imperfections. Check for holes, discoloration, and open seams, all of which are often undetectable on the rack. If you do come across a flaw, you may still be able to use the item for your purposes. Can you work around the flaw? Patch it, stitch it back together, sew an embellishment over it? By trying something on, you can walk away with a purchase—or walk away *from* a purchase—confident that you made the best choice.

Close inspection is doubly important for linens—sheets, curtains, blankets, comforters, and the like. Spread an item you're interested in on a flat surface, such as a table in the furniture section, and inspect closely for wear, tear, spots, and overall quality before deciding whether to buy.

Be prepared to leave empty-handed. I've been taking my six-year-old son, Jack, with me on my weekly thrift-store trips for a few years now. He loves searching through the toy aisle for his own treasures. He's become a thrifting pro! I call days when we find an abundance of treasures our "jackpot" days. But sometimes, we both leave the thrift store with nothing. It's a good lesson to learn, and a good one to teach as well. Just because you visit a store doesn't mean you are required to buy.

design Diversions

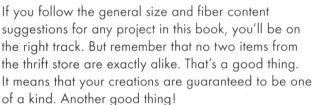

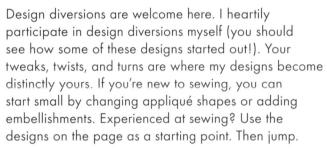

If you follow the general size and fiber content suggestions for any project in this book, you'll be on the right track. But remember that no two items from the thrift store are exactly alike. That's a good thing. It means that your creations are guaranteed to be one of a kind. Another good thing!

Design diversions are welcome here. I heartily participate in design diversions myself (you should see how some of these designs started out!). Your tweaks, twists, and turns are where my designs become distinctly yours. If you're new to sewing, you can start small by changing appliqué shapes or adding embellishments. Experienced at sewing? Use the designs on the page as a starting point. Then jump.

You'll find a "Design Diversion" section for all of the projects in *ReSew*. That's where I share things I could've done, should've done, wanted to try, thought about, or imagined. (Or, yes, even dreamed about.) Perhaps some of the ideas I would have liked to pursue will work their way into your finished projects.

SLEEVELESS V

What to do with a sweatshirt? Almost everyone I know has a few in the closet, and their families, friends, neighbors, and acquaintances have a stash in their closets. Most thrift shops are overflowing with these comfy, casual pullovers in every size and color. (If you can't find them in the women's or men's shirts sections, check for a sportswear section.)

Yep, sweatshirts sure are easy to come by. They're also kinda boring.

To smarten up an ordinary sweatshirt, I incorporated a quilt-inspired motif that I love. The knit-style fabric that most sweatshirts are made from is really easy to work with—it's cozy-soft, has a nice, chunky weight, is pliable and resilient, and doesn't fray. As you cut apart your sweatshirt and sew up this textured tank, I encourage you to take the design in your own direction. Decide what kind of details *you* want to create; then get down to transforming that plain Jane sweatshirt!

my fiber facts

Size: Women's Large

Content: 50% cotton, 50% polyester

design diversions

- Scoop neckline
- Zigzags or curves in the strips
- Softer design motifs, such as circles or flowers
- Design motif on the pocket
- Write "I MADE THIS" in strips!

GATHER YOUR MATERIALS

- One roomy* sweatshirt in your favorite color
- Thread to match sweatshirt fabric
- A favorite fitted shirt (with or without sleeves, to use as a pattern)
- Fabric-marking tool
- Long pins
- Scissors and/or rotary-cutting equipment
- Ruler or other straight edge
- Freezer paper
- Washable glue stick

Make sure the sweatshirt does not have raglan sleeves. Raglan sleeves have a diagonal seam that runs from the underarm to the neckline.

RETIP   a custom fit

If you don't have a favorite shirt to use as a guide to create a custom fit, try this. Cut away just the sleeves from the sweatshirt, turn it inside out, and try it on. Use safety pins to pin along the side seams, creating a formfitting shape you like. Remove the sweatshirt, lay it on a flat surface, and draw a line ¼" outside the safety pins. Pin the sweatshirt layers together ½" inside the drawn lines; then cut along the drawn line. Remove first set of safety pins for sewing a ¼" seam allowance.

SLEEVELESS V

CUT AND SEW THE SWEATSHIRT

1. Turn the sweatshirt inside out and lay it flat, front side up. Use scissors to carefully cut the sleeves away from the body of the sweatshirt, including any seams. Set the sleeves aside; you'll use them later. Lay a close-fitting shirt of your own on top of the sweatshirt, matching the shoulder seams. Trace the shirt shape onto the sweatshirt, from the seams under the arms to the bottom hem, using a marking tool. Trace the armholes or trace the armhole seams by folding the sleeve under along the seam. Remove the shirt. Pin both sweatshirt layers together about ½" inside the drawn lines.

2. Cut out the shape ¼" beyond the drawn lines to add a seam allowance. Cut off the bottom band of the sweatshirt and trim the lower edge to the length you want for your tank. If you want your tank to be the same length as the close-fitting shirt you're using as a pattern, cut the bottom of the sweatshirt to the same length as the shirt.

   Note: As you cut, be sure to keep as much sweatshirt fabric intact as possible. You'll need long strips for appliquéing later. ❶

3. Sew the side seams of the tank shape along the drawn lines, right sides together. Backstitch at both ends. Leave the armholes and bottom of the shirt open. Remove any remaining pins.

4. Turn the tank right side out and lay flat. On the front of the tank, find and mark the center point between the bottoms of each armhole. This will be the bottom of the V-neck opening. ❷

5. Using a ruler or other straight edge, draw a straight line from the marked center point to the shoulder on each side of the neck opening, outside of any ribbing. ❸

6. Cut the V-neck opening in the tank front and trim away the ribbing around the entire neck opening. Try on the tank and adjust the neckline if desired.

SEW THE POCKET

1. Fold the freezer paper in half shiny sides together and trace the pocket pattern (page 18) onto the freezer paper. Cut out the shape and unfold to make a complete template.

2. Cut one sweatshirt sleeve open along the seam and lay it flat. Place the freezer-paper template on the sleeve, shiny side down, and align the arrow on the template with the straight of grain. Press the freezer-paper template to the fabric with a dry iron. Cut out the pocket along the edges of the paper. Gently remove the freezer paper. ❹

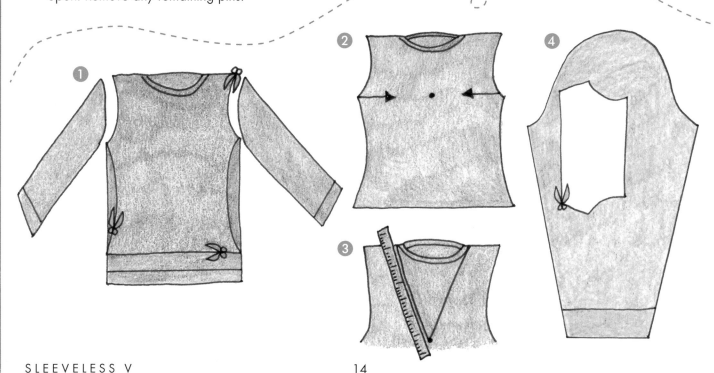

3. Cut the other sleeve open along the seam and lay it flat, right side up. Cut away any ribbing at the bottom of the sleeve. Following the straight of grain, straighten one long edge in preparation for cutting ½"-wide strips. Cut as many ½"-wide strips as you can from the length of the sleeve using a rotary cutter, ruler, and mat or scissors. **5**

4. Lay the pocket on a flat surface. Lay a ½"-wide strip from step 3 across the top of the pocket, aligning the edges. Cut the strip to fit the pocket width. Dot the strip with glue stick on the wrong side and finger-press it in place. Sew ⅛" from the edge across the bottom of the strip. Repeat for the *bottom* of the pocket, but sew ⅛" from the *top* of the strip. **6**

Note: Select the shortest ½"-wide strip that will work for each step. Save the longest strips for the neckline and the bottom of your tank.

5. Cut two strips to match the lengths of the two short, angled sides of the pocket. Align the edges and glue in place. Sew ⅛" from the *inside* edge of each strip, closer to the pocket center. **7**

6. Repeat step 5 to attach strips to the curved sides of the pocket, but this time, sew ⅛" from *both* sides of each strip. **8**

7. Position the pocket 2" above the bottom front of the shirt and center it from side to side. Glue or pin in place. Sew along the bottom and angled sides of the pocket ⅛" from the edge. Backstitch at the beginning and end of your stitching. Repeat for the top of the pocket. Leave the curved edges open. **9**

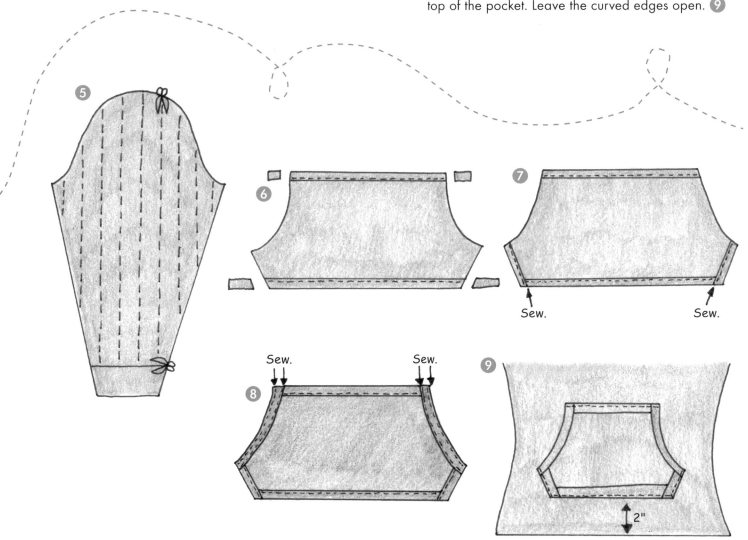

Sew.   Sew.

Sew.   Sew.

2"

ADD THE DETAILS

1. Choose the longest remaining ½"-wide strip. Pin or glue the strip around the neckline, starting a scant ½" below one side of the lower point of the V opening. (I started on what is my left side when I'm wearing the tank.) Glue the strip in place up around the neck opening and down the other side of the V, over the beginning of the strip, and diagonally down to the pocket. Cut the strip flush with the top of the pocket. **10**

2. Beginning on the side of the strip that is farther away from the edge of the neckline, sew from the beginning of the strip to the end, ⅛" from the edge. Repeat along the opposite side of the strip, closest to the edge of the neckline. Backstitch at the beginning and end of your stitching. **11**

3. Using the same method as in step 1, sew a ½"-wide strip around each armhole. However, sew the side of the strip that is closer to the edge of the armhole first and sew the side of the strip farther from the edge last. Start and end the strip at the side seam. Backstitch at the beginning and end of your stitching. **12**

RETIP *joining strips*

If you don't have enough fabric to make one continuous strip, you can butt the ends of two shorter strips in an inconspicuous place, such as at the back center of the neckline or at a side seam. Sew them as if they were one continuous strip. And don't forget—you can cut additional strips from any leftover sweatshirt fabric if you need more.

4. In the same manner, sew a ½"-wide strip around the bottom of the tank. Sew the side of the strip closer to the tank bottom edge first; sew the side of the strip farther from the edge last. Start and end strips at the side seams. Backstitch at the beginning and end of your stitching. **13**

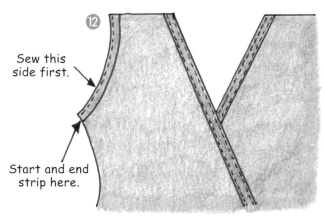

10 Start here. End here.

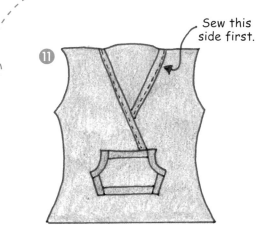

11 Sew this side first.

12 Sew this side first. Start and end strip here.

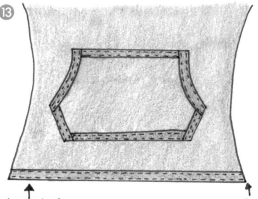

13 Sew this side first. Start and end strips at side seams.

LOG CABIN SQUARES

1. Lay the tank flat, right side out and front side up. From a remaining ½"-wide strip, cut one ½" square. This will be the center of the largest Log Cabin motif. Position the square where you want it to be on the tank (I placed mine on a slight angle); glue in place. From a remaining strip, cut a second ½" square. Place it below the square on the tank and glue in place. Cut a ½" x 1" rectangle and align one long edge with the squares. Glue in place.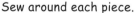

2. Lay a strip along the top edge of the square shape, bumping the edges together. Cut the strip to the length of the square shape; glue in place. Working clockwise, continue cutting and gluing strips around the square shape until the shape is five strips wide (a total of nine pieces). Sew ⅛" from the edge around all four sides of the squares and rectangle strips. Start at the center and move outward, lifting your presser foot and moving from strip to strip. ⑮

3. Repeat steps 1 and 2 to create two smaller Log Cabin motifs above and below the large Log Cabin motif. Use five pieces for each smaller motif. ⑯

4. Follow the sweatshirt manufacturer's instructions to wash and dry your tank top. Running your tank top through a machine dryer cycle will cause the raw edges of the strips and Log Cabin squares to lift off the tank, creating a fluffy, fun texture.

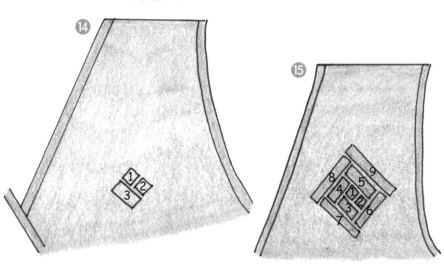

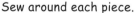

Sew around each piece.

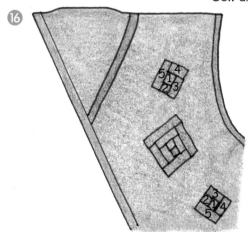

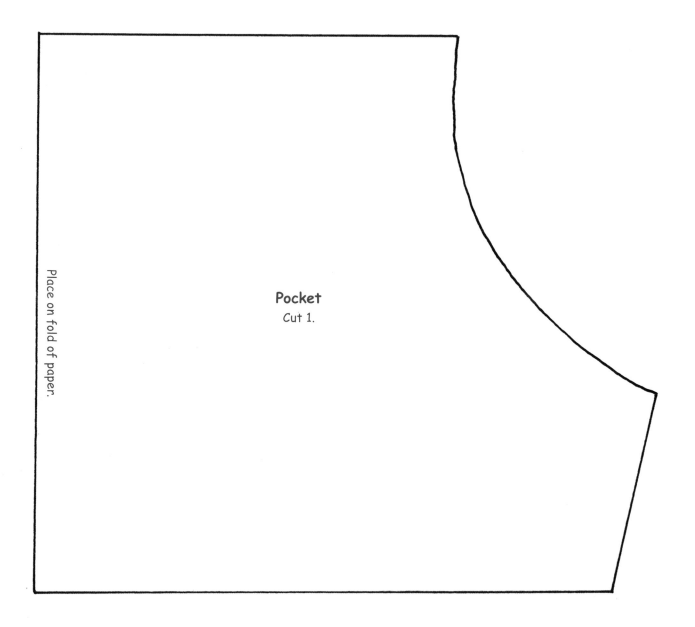

Place on fold of paper.

Pocket
Cut 1.

wraparound SHIRT

Sweatshirts are quite plentiful at thrift stores, so I explored a lot of possibilities for them when I was writing this book. With this design, I was working toward something asymmetrical and playful. And this little tank? I tried on the final design with a beautiful, rust-colored beaded necklace I received as a gift long ago. The combination instantly turned me into one hot mama. (If I do, most humbly, say so myself. I am a mama of two, after all.)

My advice? Make this one up and save it for a springtime date night.

my fiber facts

Size: Mens 2X

Content: 50% cotton, 50% polyester

design diversions

- "Wrap" both of the straps instead of just one
- Don't "wrap" at all—keep the design in the style of a traditional tank top
- Add seed beads in a matching color along the edges of each diagonal stripe
- Weave strips horizontally and vertically
- Try the design with a T-shirt instead of a sweatshirt

GATHER YOUR MATERIALS

- One roomy sweatshirt* in your favorite color
- A favorite fitted shirt (with or without sleeves, to use as a pattern)**
- Fabric-marking tool
- Scissors and/or rotary-cutting equipment
- Long pins
- Long ruler or book
- Washable glue stick
- Cardstock, light cardboard, or heavy paper
- Dinner plate

*Make sure the sweatshirt does not have raglan sleeves. Raglan sleeves have a diagonal seam that runs from the underarm to the neckline.

**If you don't have a close-fitting shirt to use as a guide, see "A Custom Fit" on page 12.

CUT AND SEW THE SWEATSHIRT

1. Turn the sweatshirt inside out and lay it flat, front side up. Use scissors to carefully cut the sleeves and waistband away from the body of the sweatshirt, including any seams. Set the sleeves aside. Lay a close-fitting shirt of your own on top of the sweatshirt, matching the shoulder seams and folding back the sleeves if necessary. Trace the shirt shape onto the sweatshirt, from the seams under the arms to the bottom hem, using a marking tool. Make a dot on the sweatshirt to mark the end of the side

seam; mark the top of the armhole opening as well. Continue drawing up to the corners of the shoulder seams on the sweatshirt. **①**

2. Remove the shirt and pin both sweatshirt layers together about ½" inside the drawn lines. Cut out the shape ¼" beyond the drawn lines to add a seam allowance. **②**

3. Sew the side seams of the tank along the drawn lines, right sides together, ending and backstitching at the arm-opening dots you made in step 1. Remove any pins and turn the sweatshirt right side out.

4. To create a gentle curve for the armholes, lay the tank out flat. Align a dinner plate, upside down, with the two dots at the armhole openings; trace a line to connect the dots. Pin the layers together and cut away the excess sweatshirt fabric. **③**

5. Place a straight edge, such as a long ruler or book, from the bottom of one armhole to the neckline on the opposite side of the sweatshirt, just below the ribbing around the neck. Draw a line along the straight edge. On the opposite side of the neckline, draw a line that is perpendicular to the first drawn line, starting just below the ribbing around the neck at the shoulder seam and ending at the first drawn line. Cut along the drawn lines, starting at the bottom of the armhole. When you reach the ribbing around the neck, cut it away around the back of the neck close to the stitching; then cut along the perpendicular line. **④**

6. Cut away the curved side of the shoulder strap so the two sides of the strap are straight and parallel to each other as shown, making the strap about 2¾" wide. **⑤**

7. Lay the shirt on a flat surface with the shoulder strap unfolded. Starting at the outside edge of the shoulder strap, begin folding and pressing the fabric to the *right* side of the shirt ¼". Continue down the arm opening, across the front, around the neck, and back up to the inside edge of the shoulder strap. Fold the

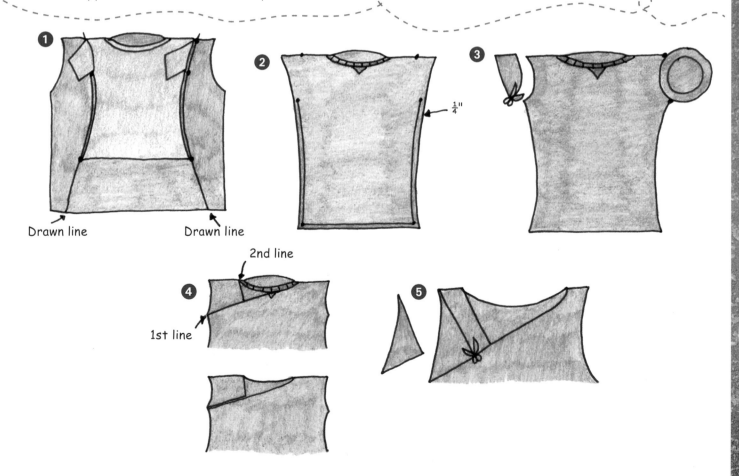

Drawn line   Drawn line

2nd line

1st line

fabric to the *right* side of the shirt ¼" again; press and pin in place. Repeat this process on the opposite arm opening and around the bottom of the shirt. **6**

8. Starting at the outside edge of the shoulder strap, sew the folded fabric down, stitching just inside the edge closest to the body of the shirt. Repeat to sew the folded fabric down on the opposite arm opening and around the bottom of the shirt. **7**

9. Try the shirt on. (Don't you look *sexy*?) Bring the strap around to the front of the shirt and pin the strap in place where it feels comfortable. The strap should tuck inside the shirt by a minimum of ½". Carefully remove the shirt. Sew across the width of the strap, just under the neckline seam, to secure the strap in place. Backstitch at the beginning and end of the seam. **8**

ADD THE STRIPES

1. Cut one sweatshirt sleeve open along the seam and lay it flat, right side up. Cut off any ribbing at the cuff. Cut the sleeve lengthwise into 1"-wide strips, discarding any strips that are less than 3" or 4" in length. **9**

2. Cut a strip of cardstock, light cardboard, or heavy paper that measures 1½" in width. Lay the strip across the top of the shirt, bumping one long edge of the paper against the neckline seam and following the diagonal direction of the neckline. With a marking tool, mark dots along the bottom of the strip of paper. **10**

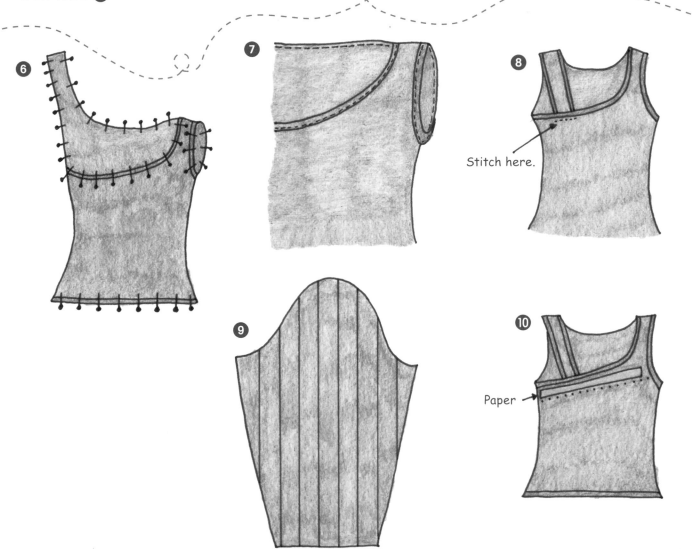

Stitch here.

Paper

3. Choose a sleeve strip that is slightly longer than the width of the front of your shirt. With the *wrong* side of the fabric facing up, align the top long edge of a sleeve strip with the dotted line, dotting the strip with glue stick and pressing it in place as you go. Carefully cut any excess strip length away so the short edges align with the side seams and/or armhole opening. Sew around the entire strip, ⅛" inside the edges of the strip. ⓫

4. Repeat steps 2 and 3 to add and sew diagonal strips until you reach the bottom of the shirt. Continue adding shorter strips in a diagonal direction until you're 1½" or less from the bottom of the shirt. ⓬

WRAPAROUND SHIRT

knit-knot T-SHIRT

Roomy, stretchy shirts like this one are plentiful at most thrift stores. They come in a rainbow of colors (both solid and multicolored), an array of patterns—like florals, stripes, and geometrics—and they can even feature sayings and designer logos. What one is your favorite? As long as the shirt stretches, the choice is yours.

my fiber facts

Size: Women's 2X

Content: 62% polyester, 34% rayon, 4% spandex

design diversions

- Scoop neck or V-neck
- Add knots to side seams
- Add another pocket
- Knot two or three rows along the neckline
- Incorporate fabric from a second shirt for knots and pockets

GATHER YOUR MATERIALS

- One long-sleeved T-shirt, roomy on the wearer
- Thread to match T-shirt fabric
- A favorite fitted shirt (with or without sleeves, to use as a pattern)
- Scissors
- Fabric-marking tool
- Long pins
- A square ruler, large flat book, or other flat object you can slide inside the shirt
- Seam ripper
- Safety pin
- Hand sewing needle
- Freezer paper

CUT AND SEW THE T-SHIRT

1. Turn the T-shirt inside out and lay it on a flat surface, front side up; smooth out wrinkles and align the bottom and side edges. With scissors, carefully cut the sleeves and sleeve seams away from the body of the T-shirt. Set the sleeves aside; you'll use them later.

2. Place your fitted shirt front side up on top of the thrifted T-shirt, aligning the shoulder seams and centering it from side to side. Use a marking tool to trace each side edge of the fitted shirt shape onto the thrifted shirt, from the sleeve seam of the fitted shirt down to the bottom of the thrifted shirt. **1**

3. Remove the fitted shirt and pin the thrifted shirt layers together ½" inside the drawn lines. Cut out the shape ¼" beyond the drawn lines. Using a ¼" seam allowance and a straight stitch (or a straight stretch stitch, if your machine has it), sew up both side seams on the drawn lines. Backstitch at the beginning and end. **2**

   Note: If the seams under the armholes don't quite match up, simply cut the longer edge so it aligns with the shorter edge at the seam. Then, cut a gentle curve that meets the outer edge of the armhole. **3**

4. Turn the shirt right side out and lay it flat. Insert a square ruler or book inside the shirt and bump the top edge against the shoulder seams. Mark the center point below the neckline between the bottoms of the armholes. Draw a vertical line down each side of the neckline, outside of the neckline seam, in line with the marked center point and bottom of the armholes. Draw a horizontal line to mark the bottom of the new neckline. Cut just outside the drawn lines to the shoulder seams; then carefully cut away any neckline seams around the back of the shirt. **4**

5. Try on the shirt. If you like the length as is, carefully cut away only the seamed hem at the bottom of the shirt. Otherwise, mark and cut the bottom edge to the desired length. Sew a straight stitch ¼" from the raw edges around the neckline, armholes, and bottom edge to stabilize the fabric. **5**

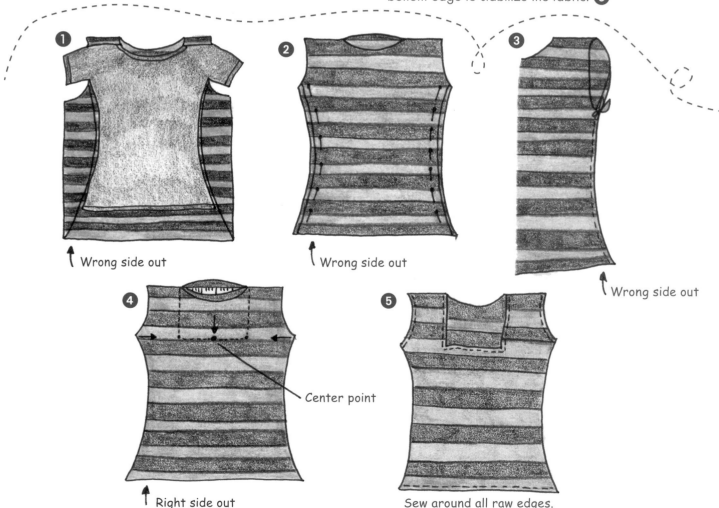

↑ Wrong side out

↑ Wrong side out

↑ Wrong side out

Center point

↑ Right side out

Sew around all raw edges.

CUT THE STRIPS, KNOT THE KNOTS

1. Cut one sleeve open along the seam and remove the cuff seam. Lay the sleeve on a flat surface and smooth out any wrinkles. Starting at the longest point of the sleeve, cut six 1"-wide strips. **6**

2. Position the shirt body so that you can work on a shoulder seam. Beginning just inside the ¼" stitching line and ¼" from one shoulder seam, mark six evenly spaced dots parallel to the shoulder seam. Repeat on the other side of the shoulder seam; then repeat on the opposite shoulder. **7**

3. With a seam ripper, make scant ¼" cuts along each dot, perpendicular to the shoulder seam. To do this, pick up a scant ¼" of fabric with the seam ripper and pull gently to cut through the fabric. **8**

4. Insert a safety pin into one short end of a strip from step 1. Insert the safety pin and strip through the first two cuts on a front shoulder seam, first in, and then out. Pull the strip through the second cut until you have a 4" tail. Tie a knot in the tail and cinch it close to the cut hole. Tie a second knot so it covers the first knot. (Don't tie the knots so they sit next to each other; tie them so they become one bigger knot.) **9**

5. Tie another two knots in the same way at the second cut. But this time, cinch the knots close enough to the shirt to gather the fabric a bit. Pull the strip through the third and fourth cuts, first in, and then out. Tie two knots, gathering the fabric. Repeat with cuts five and six. You will have a total of four knots. **10**

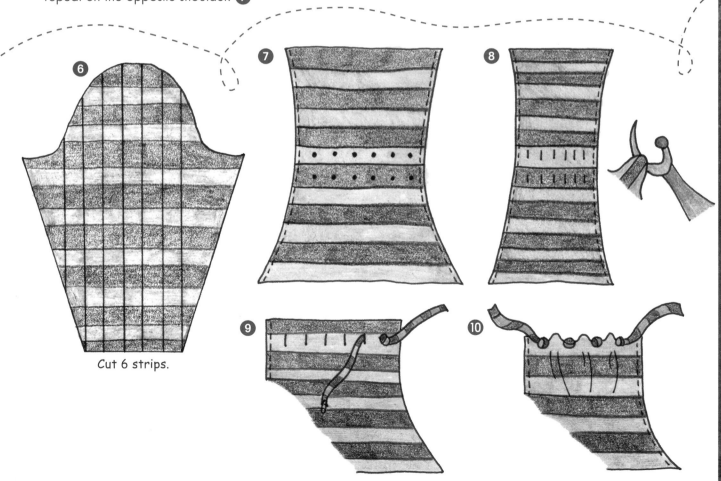

Cut 6 strips.

6. Repeat steps 4 and 5 with the back shoulder-seam cuts, and then with the front and back shoulder-seam cuts on the opposite side. Use a new strip from step 1 for each shoulder seam.

7. Using the seam ripper as in step 3, make an *even number* of evenly spaced vertical cuts along the lower edge of the neckline on the wrong side, starting directly below the vertical stitching and ¼" down from the horizontal stitching. Then repeat steps 4 and 5 to tie doubled knots along the neckline, gathering fabric as you go. (I made 16 holes and tied 10 knots.) ⓫

8. Try on your shirt. Do you like the strip tails? If so, great—you can leave them as is or cut them to a length you like. If you prefer the look of just the knots, thread a hand sewing needle with matching thread; knot the end. Fold a strip tail in half lengthwise and pull it so the part that comes out of the knot is hidden behind the knot. Take a few hand stitches to secure the strip to the knot. Cut the strip tails about ⅛" from each knot. ⓬

MAKE AND ATTACH THE POCKET

1. Trace the pocket pattern (page 29) onto the dull side of the freezer paper. Cut out the shape to make a template.

2. Cut the second sleeve open along the seam; lay the sleeve on a flat surface and smooth out any wrinkles. Place the freezer-paper template on the sleeve, shiny side down, and press with a dry iron. Cut out the shape just outside the edges of the paper. Gently remove the freezer paper and stay stitch ¼" from the raw edge of the pocket opening (the concave portion of the moon shape).

3. As with the shoulder seams and neckline, cut 10 evenly spaced vertical slits along the pocket opening, starting ¼" from one side edge and ¼" below the stay stitching. Use the remaining 1"-wide strip and tie knots as you did before to gather the top of the pocket, except tie only one knot each time; do not make double knots. You should end up with six single knots. If you want to hand sew and cut the strip tails, do so now. I liked the tails on my pocket, so I cut them both to the same length and left them on. ⓭

⓫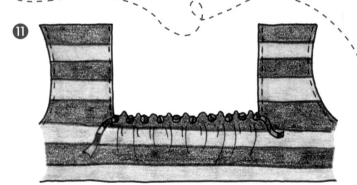

⓬

Back of knot

⓭

4. Place the pocket on your shirt in a spot you like; pin in place. Sew a straight stitch ¼" from the pocket edges, leaving the top edge open. (If the knots are in the way of your presser foot when machine sewing, simply move the knot to the left with your finger and sew past the knot.) 14

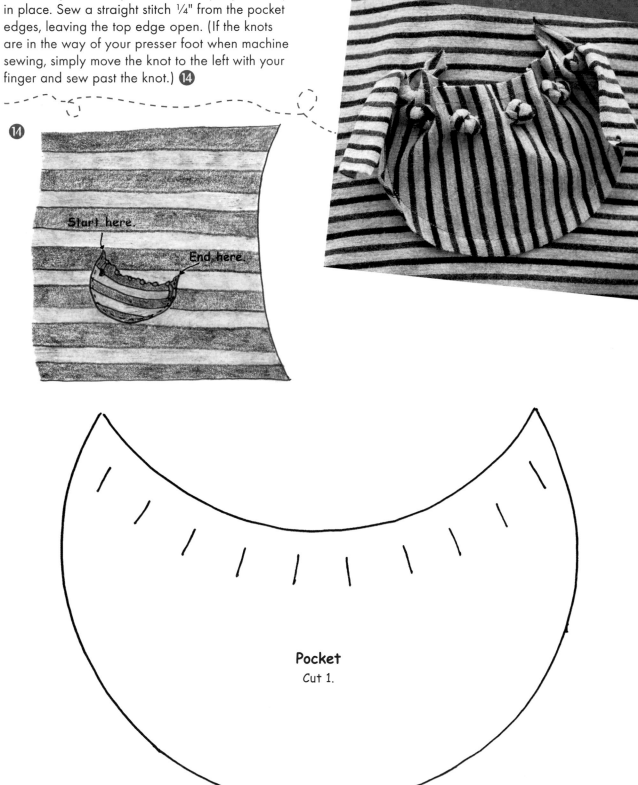

14

Start here.

End here.

Pocket
Cut 1.

two-tee TANK TOP

The shirts you choose for this flirty summer top should be of a T-shirt–style material. A mix of fibers, such as cotton, spandex, or polyester, is okay. Just make sure the fabric is knit, not woven; otherwise, the raw edges will fray.

To follow the pattern exactly, you'll need to choose shirts that measure at least 16½" wide across the front, so pack your dressmaker's measuring tape for this thrift-store trip. However, if you have a shirt that's not quite that wide, you can narrow the width of your straps to make the design work.

my fiber facts

Size: Women's Medium, Women's Large

Content: 100% cotton

design diversions

- Spaghetti straps
- Squares instead of rectangles to make the straps
- No straps!
- Hem the bottom edge
- Appliqué flowers over flowers in the fabric, using the opposite-colored shirt fabrics

GATHER YOUR MATERIALS

- Two coordinating T-shirts (shirts should differ in pattern but share a bit of the same color)
- Thread to coordinate with shirts
- 1"-wide elastic to fit loosely around your torso above your bust
- Scissors and/or rotary-cutting equipment
- Dressmaker's measuring tape
- Cardstock, flattened cereal box, or other heavy paper
- Safety pins
- Long pins

CUT AND SEW THE SHIRTS

1. Lay one T-shirt on a flat surface. Smooth out any wrinkles, making sure seams lie flat and bottom edges are aligned. Use scissors or rotary-cutting equipment to cut away the bottom hem of the shirt. Measure and cut a 12½"-wide rectangle from the bottom of the shirt to the neckline through

TWO-TEE TANK TOP

both layers. Cut the rectangle as long as you can. Repeat with the other shirt for total of four rectangles. **1**

2. Stack the four rectangles on a flat surface, aligning the bottom and side edges. Using the top edge of the shortest rectangle as a guide, cut all the rectangles to the same length. Cut the stack in half lengthwise for eight rectangles total. **2**

3. Alternating the patterned fabrics, sew the rectangles together along the long edges, *wrong* sides together. Use a ¼" seam allowance and a straight stitch. Backstitch at the beginning and end of each seam. Join the end rectangles in the same manner to form a tube. Press all seam allowances to one side. **3**

4. Fold and press the top edge of the tube 1¼" toward the *wrong* side; refer to "Clever Casings" (on the facing page) to make this easy and accurate. Choose one rectangle for the center front of your tank top; then mark the *back* center rectangle with a safety pin. Sew a straight stitch a scant ¼" from the raw edge of the casing, leaving a 2" opening along the center back rectangle. Backstitch at the beginning and end. **4**

5. Wrap the 1"-wide elastic above your bust in the position you want your top to rest (you'll want a snug fit). Add 1" and cut the elastic to this length. Follow "Inserting Elastic" (on the facing page) to gather the top edge.

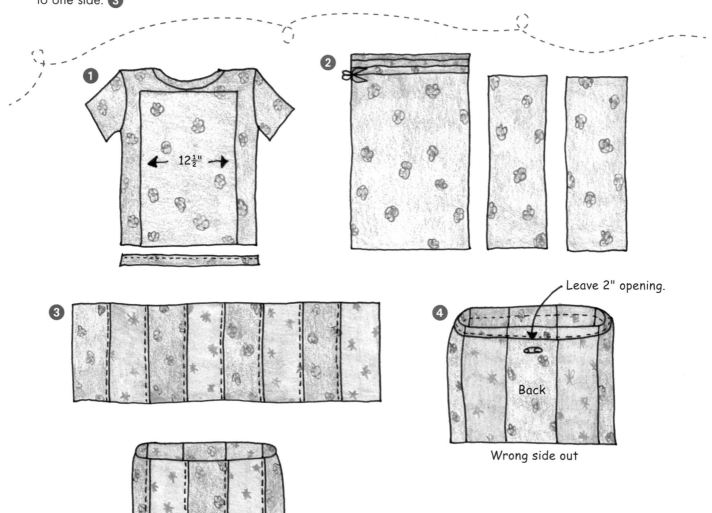

Leave 2" opening.

Back

Wrong side out

To get the measurement for a casing just right, I like-to cut a strip of heavyweight paper to the fold-over measurement. Sometimes I use both layers of a manila envelope, cut on the fold. A strip from an old folder or a flattened cereal box also works.

1. Cut the longest edge of a piece of heavyweight paper into a strip that measures 1¼" wide (or the width of your casing).

2. With the garment wrong side out, position the paper strip parallel to and about 1¼" down from the top edge. Fold the fabric over the strip so the top edge of the fabric aligns with the bottom edge of the strip; press with a dry iron or use a little steam if desired. (Steam gives a nice crease but will eventually cause the paper to curl. However, you can easily replace the paper.)

3. Continue moving the paper strip along the edge of the tube and pressing until you have folded and pressed 1¼" all around the top of the tube.

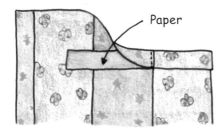

Paper

Here's how I insert elastic into casings to create gathers:

1. Insert a large safety pin through one end of the elastic two times (insert the point in and out twice) and close the pin. Push the safety pin through the casing opening. Gather fabric onto the safety pin; then pull the fabric past the pin and onto the elastic. Take care not to twist the elastic.

2. Continue pushing and pulling the elastic through the casing until the safety pin reaches the opening on the other side of the casing. Be sure you don't pull the other end of the elastic inside the casing. To prevent this from happening, you can safety pin the other end of the elastic to the outside of the casing.

3. Pull the casing fabric away from the elastic ends by a few inches on each side. Overlap both short ends of the elastic by ½". Using a straight stitch, sew a rectangle shape through both layers of the elastic to join the ends securely.

4. Push the elastic back into the casing. Pull the fabric taut along the 2" opening and machine sew the opening closed a scant ¼" from the raw edge; backstitch at the beginning and end. Distribute the gathers evenly.

CUT AND SEW THE STRAPS

1. Try on your tube top, adjusting it so the front rectangle rests in the middle of your chest. Safety pin the end of your dressmaker's measuring tape to the top, 1" from one edge of the center rectangle and 1" down from the top of the casing. Rotate the tube around your body 180° so the center *back* rectangle rests in the middle of your chest. Pull the measuring tape over your shoulder and pull it taut outside of the tube, 1" from the edge of the center *back* rectangle. Note the measurement where the tape hits the stitching line of your casing. This is the measurement you will use for the length of your straps. (My measurement was 17".) **5**

2. Divide your measurement roughly into thirds, rounding down to the nearest ¼". In my example: 17" ÷ 3 = 5.66"; rounded down to the nearest ¼" = 5½".

3. Cut six strips, 1½" x the length determined in step 2, from the remaining fabric of *each* shirt. (Cut the sleeves open if the leftover fabric from the front and back isn't enough.) You'll have a total of 12 strips. **6**

4. Arrange the strips into four groups of three strips each, alternating the patterned fabrics. With right sides together, sew the strips together end to end using a ¼" seam allowance to form four long strips. Press as indicated by the arrows in the illustration. **7**

5. Layer two strips *wrong* sides together. Pin. Sew ¼" from the edge all around. Repeat to make two straps. **8**

6. Pin one short edge of a strap to the inside front of the tube, 1" from one edge of the center rectangle and 1" down from the top of the casing (as you did with the measuring tape). Pin, keeping gathers in place.

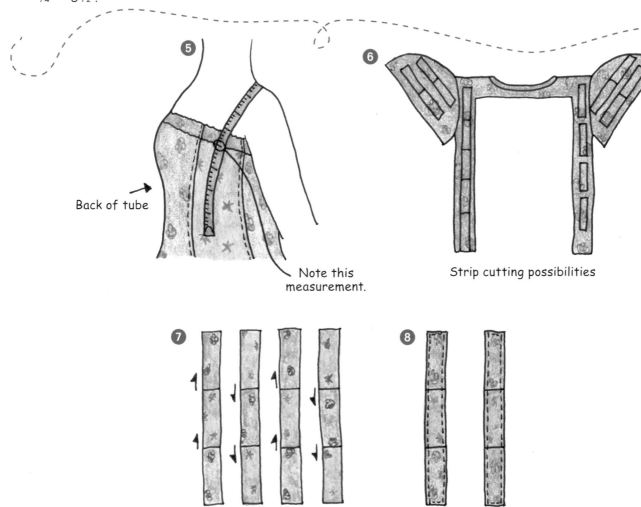

Back of tube

Note this measurement.

Strip cutting possibilities

Sew two vertical lines along each long edge of the strap, from the top of the casing to the stitching at the bottom of the casing. Repeat to attach the other end of the strap to the back of the tube. **9**

7. Repeat step 6 to attach the second strap.

CUT AND SEW THE APPLIQUÉS

1. From the leftover shirt fabric, cut four 1½" x 5" rectangles from *each* shirt, for a total of eight rectangles.

2. Pin the rectangles to the bottom of each panel around the tube, about ½" above the bottom edge and centered from side to side within each panel. Be sure to alternate the colors of the rectangles on the panels. Sew each rectangle to the tube ¼" from the raw edges. **10**

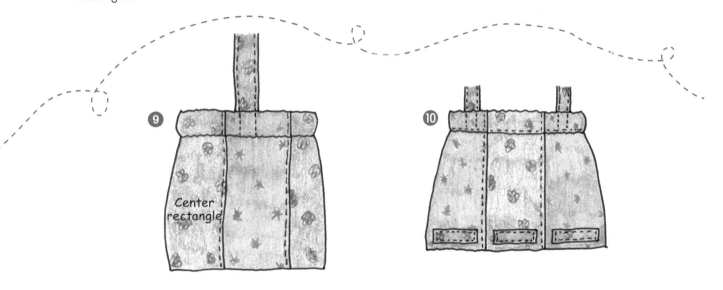

curtain SKIRT

This skirt is very simple to sew and makes a great starter project if you're new to sewing. Made from sheer curtains, it's almost as light as air to wear, but the gathers at the waist make it feel full and flouncy. In this design, the *length* of the curtain goes around your waist; you'll cut the *width* of the curtain to the finished length of your skirt. If you want to feel that extra flounce when you wear it, buy the longest curtains you can find.

my fiber facts

Size: 60" x 80"

Content: 100% polyester

design diversions

- Cut the strips in half widthwise and sew twice as many strip layers
- Build in a lightweight slip (it is sheer fabric, after all . . .)
- Add a circular or floral motif on each strip with hand sewn seed beads
- Double up the strips so you don't need a slip
- Make the skirt a sand-skimming ankle length

GATHER YOUR MATERIALS

- Two matching sheer or lightweight curtain panels, approximately 60" x 80" each (a standard curtain measurement—yours need only be in the vicinity)
- Sewing thread to match fabric
- 1"-wide elastic to fit comfortably around your waist
- Scissors and/or rotary-cutting equipment
- Dressmaker's measuring tape
- Fabric-marking tool
- Long pins
- Large safety pin

CUT THE CURTAINS

1. Spread both curtain panels on a flat surface and cut off all hems using scissors or a rotary cutter, ruler, and mat. Fold one panel in half lengthwise and press using an iron set for the fiber content of your curtains. Cut down the center of the fold to make two long rectangles of the same size. These are the front and back of your skirt.

2. Fold one long edge of one rectangle 1¼" to the wrong side for the waistband casing; press and pin. You'll be trimming this edge later, so the fold measurement doesn't have to be exact.

3. Wrap the long front rectangle around your body, holding the folded edge exactly where you want the waistband to sit. Use a dressmaker's measuring tape to measure from the top of the folded edge to where you want the hem of the skirt to fall.

CURTAIN SKIRT

Remove the rectangle from your body and trim it to that measurement. Note that the lower edge is not hemmed, so you do not need to add a hem allowance. Your height, along with where you want your hem to fall, will determine your final measurement. (My final measurement was 25" and hits right below my knee.) ❶

Note: Keep the excess fabric you cut away. You may need it for skirt panels later.

4. Repeat step 2 for the back rectangle and trim it to the length determined in step 3.

5. Cut ten 5"-wide strips from the *length* of the back. (You may need to cut more strips later. I ended up using twelve, but let's start with ten.)

SEW THE SKIRT

1. Sew ½" from the bottom edge of both rectangles for the skirt front and back. Sew ½" away from one long edge of *each* 5"-wide strip. This stitching is mostly decorative, but it will also help prevent fraying. ❷

2. With right sides of the fabric up, measure and mark 3" from the bottom of the front skirt panel. Place the bottom of one 5" strip along the marked line, aligning the edges of the strips with the edges of the panel. Pin the top of the strip to the panel. Mark and sew ½" from the top of the first strip. ❸

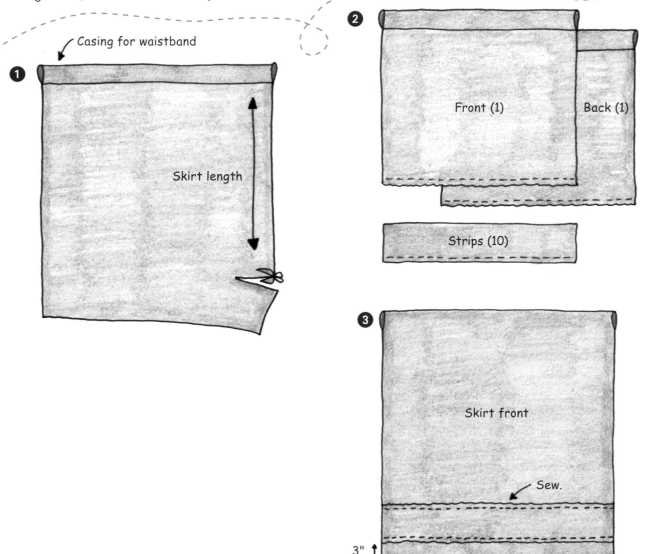

Casing for waistband

❶ Skirt length

❷ Front (1) Back (1)

Strips (10)

❸ Skirt front

Sew.

3"

3. Measure and mark 3" from the bottom of the first strip you sewed onto the front skirt panel. Place the bottom of the second strip along the marked line, aligning edges of strips with the edges of the panel. The second strip will overlap the first strip by 2". Pin the top of the second strip to the panel. Mark and sew ½" from the top of the second strip. ❹

4. Keep adding strips in this manner until the top edge of the last strip is less than 5" from the beginning of the casing. If you have used five strips on the front panel and need to add more, cut them from the second curtain panel or the remaining fabric from the first panel. Be sure to cut extra strips in pairs, one for the front skirt panel and one for the back skirt panel. ❺ ❻

5. Repeat steps 2–4 to sew strips to the back skirt panel.

6. Unfold the casing on both panels and lay the panels flat. With scissors or a rotary cutter, ruler, and mat, cut and straighten the side edges of both panels. ❼

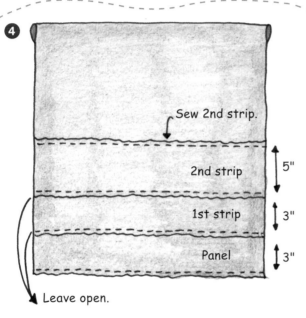

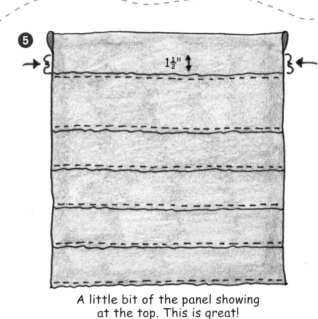

A little bit of the panel showing at the top. This is great!

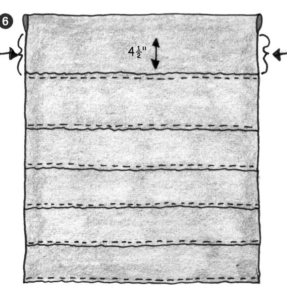

More panel showing at the top— this is great, too!

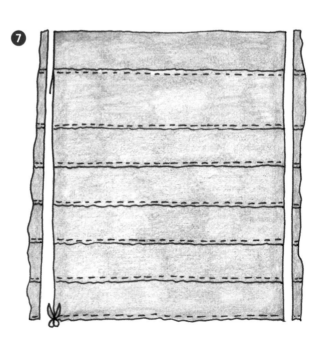

CURTAIN SKIRT

7. With a zigzag stitch, sew the side raw edges of each panel to prevent fraying. Pin the loose short edges of the 5"-wide strips down so that you don't create any pleats or folds as you sew.

8. With right sides together, pin one side edge of the front panel to one side edge of the back panel. Match the bottom edges first; then match up the 5" strips. Using a straight stitch, sew just inside your zigzag stitch. Keep the casing unfolded when sewing. **8**

9. Repeat step 8 to sew the other two sides of the panels together to form a tube.

10. Trim and straighten the top edge of the tube as in step 6, if needed. Using a zigzag stitch, sew around the top edge of the tube to prevent fraying.

11. Fold and pin the casing back in place, re-pressing the new side seams. Refer to "Clever Casings" (page 33) for easy and accurate construction. Using a straight stitch and starting at a side seam, sew the casing just inside your zigzag seam. Leave a 2" opening to insert the elastic. Backstitch at both ends.

12. Wrap the 1"-wide elastic around your waist where you want the top of the skirt to sit (you'll want a snug fit). Add 1"-wide and cut the elastic to this measurement. Follow the instructions for "Inserting Elastic" (page 33) to gather the waistband.

13. Follow the original manufacturer's care-tag instructions for washing your skirt. Because the edges are meant to be frayed, I washed and dried my skirt by machine and then trimmed the loose threads.

Wrong side of panel

cuffed SKIRT

Jeralyn Miller, a kind neighbor and friend of mine, turned me on to trying a design with men's dress pants. While walking our children to school one day, Jeralyn told me that in high school she and her friends would cut off thrifted men's dress pants at the knee, zigzag around the edges, and wear them as shorts to school.

Well, holy fashion statement. How very punk rock.

I thought my "design diversion" from Jeralyn's idea was going to be a bit punk rock too. Instead, I wound up with a surprisingly elegant, dressy skirt. And it's no wonder. While thrifting, I found dozens of beautiful blue, brown, gray, green, and tan trousers to choose from, all with lovely yet subtle patterns. The most common dress-pant fabrics will give a graceful drape and swing to this skirt. But I also came across heavier wool fabrics with check and herringbone weaves. These types of fabrics will give an entirely different look to your skirt.

Within a week of telling me her story, Jeralyn had been to the thrift store and back and had created an absolutely gorgeous skirt for her daughter. It was made entirely of men's ties, complete with a zigzagged hem that followed the shape of each tie tip. Well, holy fashion statement. Again. Passed on from mom to daughter. Jeralyn, you still rock.

my fiber facts

Size: Men's 41 Long, Men's 34/36

Content: 100% stretch wool, 100% polyester

design diversions

- Try bulkier wools for a warm winter skirt
- Choose two pairs of cuffed pants for a cuff along the entire bottom hem
- Cut pant legs in half lengthwise for a more varied, stripy look

GATHER YOUR MATERIALS

- Two coordinating pairs of men's dress pants—one with cuffs, one without
- Thread to coordinate with pants
- 1"-wide elastic to fit comfortably around your waist
- Scissors
- Dressmaker's measuring tape
- Rotary-cutting equipment
- Long pins
- Large safety pin

CUT THE PANTS

1. Spread both pairs of pants on a flat surface and cut closely along the inner and outer pant leg seams with scissors. Cut along the waistband, leaving all seaming behind. You should end up with eight pant-leg pieces that look somewhat like the illustration below. **1**

2. To determine the skirt length, fold down the top edge of one pant leg 1¼" and pin to make a temporary casing. Hold the folded edge at your waist, exactly where you want your waistband to sit. Use a dressmaker's measuring tape to measure from the top folded edge to where you want the hem of your skirt to fall. Add 1¼" to this measurement. Your height, along with where you want your hem to fall, will determine your final measurement. (My final measurement was 25" and hits right below my knee.)

3. Using the length determined in step 2, measure from the *bottom* of the pant leg and cut away the *top* of the pant leg. This preserves the bottom hems of the pants so we won't have to hem the skirt. Cut all eight pant leg pieces in the same way. **2**

4. Using a rotary cutter, mat, and ruler and starting at the narrowest part of one pant leg, trim the long sides to form a rectangle. Repeat for the other seven pant-leg pieces. Cut the widest rectangle that you can from each piece. If there are stripes in your pants, you can follow the stripes to cut your rectangles. After you've completed the cutting, you should have four narrow rectangles and four wider rectangles. (The widths are different because the back pant leg is always wider than the front.) **3**

SEW THE SKIRT

1. Lay out your rectangles in the order shown. **4**

2. Pin the rectangles right sides together, taking care to pin the cuffs so they lie flat for sewing. Starting from the bottom hems of the pant legs, use a ¼" seam allowance and a straight stitch to sew the

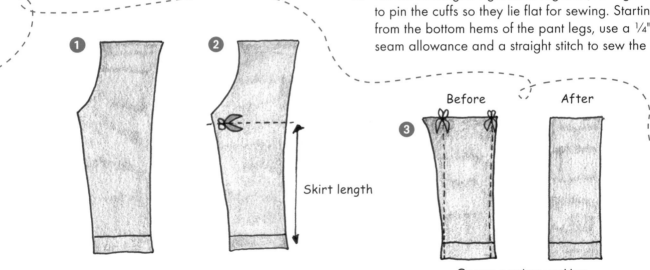

Skirt length

Before   After

Or use a rotary cutter

W = wide   N = narrow

rectangles together. When all eight pant legs are sewn into a row, sew a final seam to create a tube. Press all seam allowances to the side and sew a zigzag stitch along the straight stitching to prevent fraying. Finally, sew a zigzag stitch around the top of the tube to prevent fraying. **5**

3. Turn the tube *wrong* side out. Fold and press the top edge of the tube 1¼" toward the *wrong* side for the waistband casing; refer to "Clever Casings" (page 33) to make this easy and accurate. Choose one rectangle as the center back of your skirt. Using a straight stitch and starting at the center back rectangle, sew the casing just inside the zigzag stitches. Leave a 2" opening to insert the elastic and backstitch at the beginning and end.

4. Wrap the 1"-wide elastic around your waist where you want the top of the skirt to sit (you'll want a snug fit). Add 1" and cut the elastic to this measurement. Follow the instructions for "Inserting Elastic" (page 33) to gather the waistband.

5. Slip into your skirt, find a romantic top, and you're ready to roll.

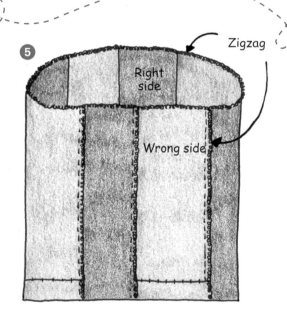

5

Zigzag

Right side

Wrong side

sheet SKIRT

The sheet I chose for this bright skirt is lightweight—no sateen-style thread counts here!—which makes it great for warm-weather wear. There's no need to limit your style to stripes; you can use solids or patterned sheets as well. If you choose a sheet that features an overall pattern, try turning the appliquéd squares in different directions around the skirt—or even using the wrong side of the fabric—so the pattern differs from the background strips.

my fiber facts

Size: 66" x 96"/twin size

Content: 100% cotton

design diversions

- Use two coordinating flat sheets, solid and patterned
- Cut square appliqués into spirals or zigzags so they visually "bounce" off the stripes
- Omit one row (but keep the hem) and make this an above-the-knee skirt
- Simplify the sewing with a traditional turned-under hem

GATHER YOUR MATERIALS

- One twin-size striped flat sheet with a large hem at the top
- Thread to match sheet fabric
- 1"-wide elastic to fit comfortably around your waist
- Scissors and/or rotary-cutting equipment
- Ruler or dressmaker's measuring tape
- Fabric-marking tool
- Long pins
- Large safety pin

CUT THE SHEET

1. Using scissors or rotary-cutting equipment, carefully cut away the large hem seam at the top of the sheet ¼" beyond the stitching. Reserve this strip for later use. Remove all remaining seams and/or selvages from the bottom and side edges of the sheet. ①

Add ¼" here.

①

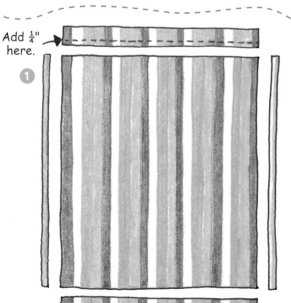

2. Cut one 11¼" x 60" strip from the sheet so the stripes are parallel to the *short* edges of the strip. This strip is for the top of the skirt. We'll call it the Top strip. Cut one 9" x 60" strip from the sheet so the stripes are parallel to the *long* edges of the strip. This strip is for the center of the skirt. We'll call it the Center strip. Cut one 9" x 60" strip from the sheet so the stripes are parallel to the *short* edges of the strip. This strip is for the bottom of the skirt. We'll call it the Bottom strip. **2**

3. From the remaining sheet fabric, cut 20 squares, 4" x 4", for appliqué and one 2½" x 60" strip with horizontal stripes for the bottom border.

MARK AND SEW THE STRIPS

1. Lay the Top strip on a flat surface. Use a ruler and marking tool to measure and mark 2¼" from one long edge, for the waistband casing. I used an air-soluble pen and marked dots every 2" or so. **3**

2. Beginning at the dots marked in step 1, measure down another 2¼" and mark dots along the length of the strip. Align the top of a 4" square with the second line of dots and place the side edge of the square 2½" from the short edge of the strip. Turn the square so the stripes run horizontally along the length of the strip. Place the second square 4½" from the first square, stripes running horizontally; pin. Continue pinning squares in the same manner across the length of the strip. You should end up pinning seven squares to the strip. **4**

3. Lay the Center strip on a flat surface. Measure 2½" from one long edge and mark dots, as in step 1. Position the Center strip below the Top strip so the short edges are aligned. Pin six squares to the Center strip as in step 2, offsetting their placement with the squares on the Top strip. Turn the squares on the Center strip so the stripes run vertically. **5**

4. Repeat step 3 with the bottom strip, pinning seven squares to the strip so that the stripes run horizontally. **6**

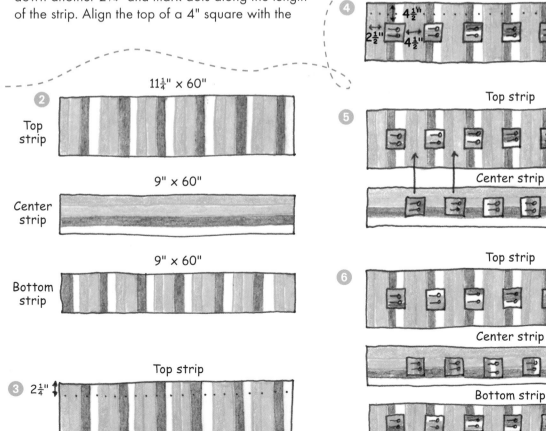

2 11¼" x 60"
Top strip

9" x 60"
Center strip

9" x 60"
Bottom strip

Top strip
3 2¼"

4 Top strip
4½"
2½" 4½"

5 Top strip
Center strip

6 Top strip
Center strip
Bottom strip

5. Sew the first square to the top strip ¼" from the edges and then sew an X from corner to corner of your stitching. Repeat to sew each square to the strips. **7**

RETIP *X marks the spot*

To make X's with straight lines, align a ruler from corner to corner diagonally across a square and mark a line with a water-soluble fabric-marking tool. Repeat with the other two corners. Sew along the lines.

SEW AND FINISH THE SKIRT

1. With *wrong* sides together, pin the bottom of the Top strip to the top of the Center strip. Stitch ¼" from the edge. Repeat to attach the bottom of the Center strip to the top of the Bottom strip. Press the seam allowances toward the bottom of the skirt. **8**

2. Using a ¼" seam allowance, sew the 2½" x 60" strip to the lower edge of the Bottom strip, *wrong* sides together.

3. To create the doubled raw-edge hem, begin by cutting the hemmed strip from the top of the sheet to 60" in length. Using a straight stitch, sew ¼" from the top folded edge of the hem. Slide the bottom blade of your scissors into the fold of the hem; carefully cut along the fold. **9**

4. Slide the bottom blade of your scissors into the opposite long edge of the hem and carefully cut along the seam. Unfold and cut away the seam hidden inside the layers of the hem. Cut and straighten both layers of the bottom of the hem, if needed. **10**

5. Place the long *unsewn* edge of the hem strip from step 4 on the wrong side of the bottom of the skirt, overlapping it by about ¼"; pin. Sew together using a straight stitch. The hem strip creates the bottom border of the skirt. As the lower edges fray, they will create a fluffy texture along the bottom. **11**

7

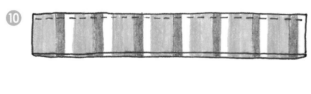
10

8
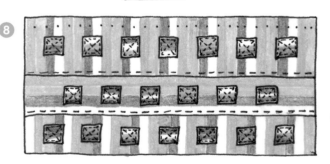

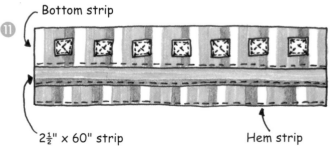

11 Bottom strip

2½" x 60" strip   Hem strip

9
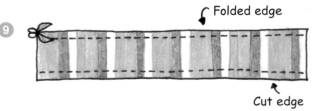

Folded edge

Cut edge

6. With right sides together, pin one side edge of the skirt to the other side edge, matching intersecting seams. Pin the raw edges of the seams toward the bottom of the skirt so they don't get folded and stitched in an upward position while sewing. Using a ¼" seam allowance, sew the skirt into a tube. **12**

7. Using a zigzag stitch, sew around the top edge of the tube to prevent fraying. Turn the tube wrong side out. Fold and press the top edge of the tube 1¼" toward the wrong side for the waistband casing; refer to "Clever Casings" (page 33) to make this easy and accurate. Pin in place. Using a straight stitch and starting at the side seam, sew the casing just inside the zigzag stitches. Leave a 2" opening to insert the elastic and backstitch at the beginning and end.

8. Wrap the 1"-wide elastic around your waist where you want the top of the skirt to sit (you'll want a snug fit). Add 1" and cut the elastic to this measurement. Follow the instructions for "Inserting Elastic" (page 33) to gather the waistband.

9. Follow the original manufacturer's care-tag instructions for washing your skirt. Because the edges are meant to be frayed, I washed and dried my skirt by machine and then trimmed the loose threads.

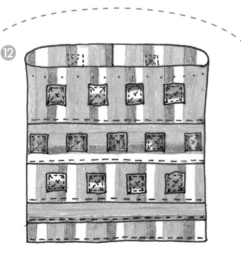

SHEET SKIRT

sweatshirt SKIRT

You wouldn't think a skirt made out of sweatshirts would make you feel like a princess. But when I first tried this finished design on, I was shocked to find myself—the only female in a four-person household—feeling quite girlie. The gathering at the top of the skirt flares the fabric outward, of course, but the weight and weave of the sweatshirt fabric makes that flare stay, well, flared. Like, all the time. It's not stiff (how could a cozy sweatshirt be stiff, after all?); the fabric simply stays exactly where the gathers put it, all the way down to the bottom. It's downright fun to wear and surprisingly feminine for a skirt made out of sweatshirts.

my fiber facts

Size: Men's Large, XL, XL

Content: 50% cotton, 50% polyester

design diversions

- Try a crazy color combo, like a mix of purple, green, and blue sweatshirts

- Turn strips into zigzags, spirals, polka dots, square dots, words, or letters

- Layer three circles (large, medium, small) on the sun motifs, instead of using only one

- Sew strips around the bottom edge of the shirt for a more finished look

- Add some beading or embroidery inside the sun

GATHER YOUR MATERIALS

- Three Large to XL sweatshirts in light, medium, and dark values of the same color (or a mix of coordinating colors)*

- Scissors and/or rotary cutter, ruler, and mat

- Dressmaker's measuring tape

- Heavy paper, cardstock, or light cardboard for making templates

- Fabric-marking tool

- Washable glue stick

- Long pins

- Sewing thread to coordinate with sweatshirt fabrics

- 1"-wide elastic to fit comfortably around your waist

- Large safety pin

- Hand sewing needle

*Ideally, your sweatshirts need to be at least as wide as two of your side-panel rectangles from "Do the Math" on page 53. This way you'll be able to cut two rectangles from the fronts and backs of each sweatshirt. If not, simply add another sweatshirt to the mix.

SWEATSHIRT SKIRT

CUT THE SWEATSHIRTS

1. Cut the waistbands off of all three sweatshirts, leaving the seams on the body of the sweatshirt (you should be able to unfold the doubled waistbands after cutting). Set aside. **❶**

2. Cut along the side seams and cut the sleeves off along the shoulder seams on all three sweatshirts; this will make cutting your skirt panels easier.

3. This skirt is constructed of two center panels and four side panels. Each center panel contains three rectangles; each side panel contains two rectangles. To determine the length and width of your rectangles, follow the formulas in "Do the Math" on page 53.

4. Cut the number of rectangles from each sweatshirt as indicated in the chart below. You can cut the sweatshirts in several ways (possibly even using the sleeves, if needed), but keep your cuts close together and toward the bottom edges to conserve as much fabric as possible. **❷**

	Center-Panel Rectangles	Side-Panel Rectangles
Light	2	4
Medium	2	2
Dark	2	2

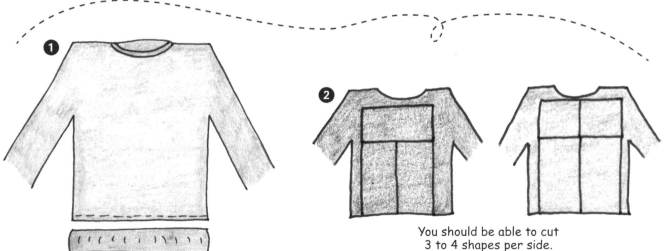

❶ Leave any seaming on body of sweatshirt.

❷ You should be able to cut 3 to 4 shapes per side.

do the math

Skirt Length

Measure from your waist to where you want the hem of your skirt to fall. (My desired length was 24" and hits right at my knee. Your height, along with where you want your hem to fall, will best determine your final measurement.) Subtract 1" for the waistband to determine your "final length measurement."

_____ - 1" = _____
Desired length   Final length measurement

My example: 24" - 1" = 23"

Now, use the "final length measurement" to determine the length to cut rectangles for the center and side panels. Use a calculator here and when dividing, round down to the nearest ¼".

Length of Center-Panel Rectangles

_____ ÷ 3 = _____; + ½" for seams = _____
Final length measurement   Length of center rectangles

My example: 23" ÷ 3 = 7.666" (round down to nearest ¼") = 7½" + ½" = 8"

Length of Side-Panel Rectangles

_____ ÷ 2 = _____; + ½" for seams = _____
Final length measurement   Length of side rectangles

My example: 23" ÷ 2 = 11½" + ½" = 12"

Width of Rectangles

Wrap your dressmaker's measuring tape around your waist exactly where you want the top of your skirt to sit. (You'll want it to be snug.) Add ½" to this measurement for seams. Double this number, then divide by six to determine the width to cut your rectangles (the rectangles are all the same width).

_____ x 2 = _____; ÷ 6 = _____ + ½" for seams = _____
Waistband measurement   Rectangle width

My example:

31" x 2 = 62"; ÷ 6 = 10.33 (round down to nearest ¼") = 10¼" + ½" = 10¾"

Yay, we're done with the math! Now you can plug in your numbers below:

Center-Panel Rectangles: _____ x _____
                          length   width

Side-Panel Rectangles: _____ x _____
                        length   width

My example:

Center-Panel Rectangles: 8" x 10¾"

Side-Panel Rectangles: 12" x 10¾"

CUT AND SEW THE APPLIQUÉS

1. Lay out the rectangles for the front of the skirt in a color arrangement you like. Or follow the diagram below. ❸

2. Using a sleeve from each sweatshirt, cut the wristbands off and cut up the sleeve seam. (If there are no sleeve seams, cut up the sleeve at its shortest length.) Cut five strips, ½" wide, from each sleeve. Cut them from each sleeve's longest point and be sure to cut along the straight of grain (following the lines of the fabric). ❹

3. Trace the circle patterns on page 57 onto cardstock, a flattened cereal box, or other heavy paper to make templates. Cut out along the drawn lines.

4. Trace the templates onto the sweatshirt material and follow the cutting chart above right. Trace the circles onto any portion of the sweatshirts that remain, including fabric left from the body of each sweatshirt and/or from the second sleeve of each garment. For circles, you don't need to worry about straight of grain, so you can cut anyhow, anywhere.

	Light	Medium	Dark
Small circle	--	--	1
Medium circle	1	1	--
Large circle	1	--	1

5. Using the circles from step 4 and the strips from step 2, create a sun-and-ray shape on the center rectangle of the center panel. Place the circle first, at least ½" from each edge. Keep the circle in place with a few dots of glue stick. To create the rays, lay one strip of a contrasting color to the background rectangle about ½" away from the circle; lay it across the rectangle to the opposite corner. Cut the strip to a length at least ½" away from the edge of the rectangle. Secure the ray in place with glue stick. Lay a second strip in a different color next to the first strip, cut to desired length, and adhere with glue stick. Repeat for the remaining rays, spacing the rays about ½" apart around the sun. ❺

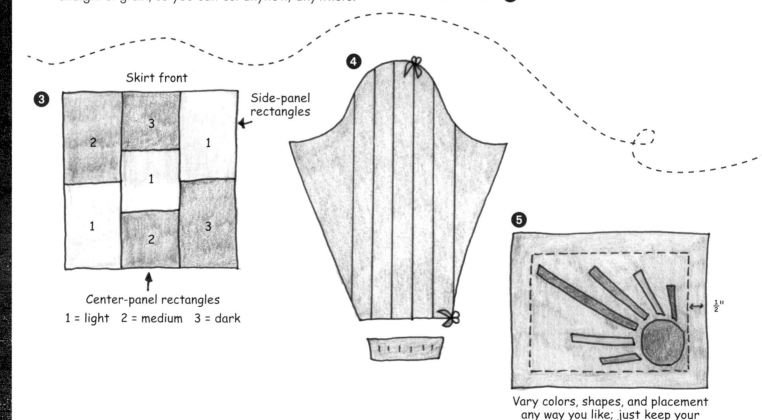

Skirt front

❸

Side-panel rectangles

3

2 1

1

1 3

2

Center-panel rectangles
1 = light   2 = medium   3 = dark

❹

❺

½"

Vary colors, shapes, and placement any way you like; just keep your design ½" inside all edges.

6. Repeat step 5 to create the suns and rays on the four side-panel rectangles. **6**

7. Beginning with the center-panel rectangle, sew the circle to the rectangle, topstitching ⅛" from the raw edges. Sew the strips to the rectangle in the same manner. Backstitch at the beginning and end of all stitching. Repeat to sew the circles and strips to the four side-panel rectangles. **7**

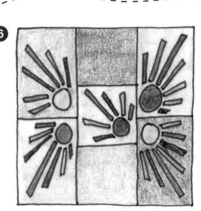

My design placement and color choices

Sew all pieces using a $\frac{1}{8}$" seam.

RETIP

easy sewing on the edge

Does sewing ⅛" from the edge sound tricky to you? I promise it won't be if you use this little trick. Using a standard presser foot, align the edge of your fabric with the right interior edge of the presser "toe," and then you can let your presser foot do the guiding.

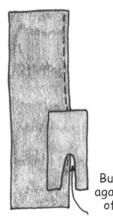

Bump fabric against inside of presser foot.

SEW THE SKIRT

1. Lay out the rectangles for the front of the skirt in order. Beginning with the center panel, pin and sew the top rectangle to the middle rectangle with wrong sides together using a ¼" seam allowance. Pin and sew the bottom rectangle to the middle rectangle in the same manner. Then, pin and sew the side-panel pieces together. **8**

2. To sew the three front-panel pieces together, find the center of the middle rectangle on the center panel. Mark the center on both sides with pins. **9**

3. With wrong sides together, match up the center seam of the left-side panel to the center of the middle rectangle; pin. Ease and pin the edges of both panels together. Sew the panels together using a ¼" seam allowance, making sure that the raw-edge seam allowances that approach your needle from the center panel are pressed and sewn toward the bottom of the skirt. Repeat to sew the right-side panel to the center panel.

4. Repeat steps 1–3 to sew the rectangles together as shown for the back of the skirt. **10**

5. With wrong sides together, match the center seams of the side panels; pin. Sew the skirt front to the skirt back, creating a tube. Again, make sure raw-edge seam allowances are folded and sewn toward the bottom of the skirt.

6. Press all seam allowances around the top of the skirt toward the center back of the skirt. Using a zigzag or overlock stitch, sew around the top of the skirt tube. (This will help keep the fabric from rolling up once the waistband is attached.)

ATTACH THE WAISTBAND

1. Choose two of the three sweatshirt waistbands to create your skirt waistband. Measure across the three panels of the skirt front; cut each band to this measurement, adding ½" for seams to each. Fold the sweatshirt bands lengthwise (as they were folded on the original sweatshirts); cut the bands lengthwise so that they are 1¼" in width, cutting through both layers.

2. Unfold both waistbands. With right sides together and using a ¼" seam allowance, sew the short ends of each waistband together. Sew both short ends of the opposite sides of the waistband together until you pass the folds in the fabric; backstitch. Lift the presser foot and move the fabric to about ¼" from the end of the fabric; sew to the end and backstitch. (You've created a 1" opening to insert the waistband elastic later.) Press the seam allowances open. Refold the waistband so the seam allowances are hidden inside. **11**

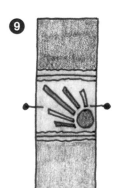

9

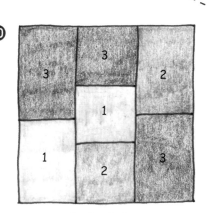

10

Back of skirt
1 = light   2 = medium   3 = dark

11

Leave hole for elastic.

3. Mark dots ½" away from the edge all the way around the top of the skirt tube. Matching the side seams of the waistband to the side seams of the skirt tube, place the doubled raw edges of the waistband on the right side of the skirt top. (Make sure the hole you created to insert the elastic is on the inside of the skirt.) Align the raw edges of the waistband with the ½" dots on the skirt; pin well. Sew the waistband to the skirt tube using a ¼" seam allowance. Backstitch at each end. **12**

4. Wrap the 1"-wide elastic around your waist exactly where you want the top of your skirt to sit (you'll want it to be snug). Add 1" and cut the elastic to this measurement. Follow "Inserting Elastic" (page 33) to gather the waistband edge of the skirt. Hand stitch the opening closed. **13**

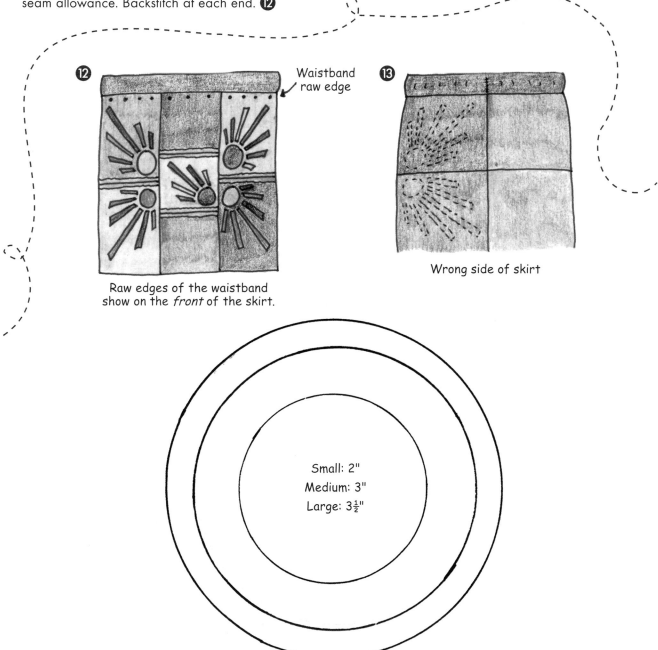

Waistband raw edge

Raw edges of the waistband show on the *front* of the skirt.

Wrong side of skirt

Small: 2"
Medium: 3"
Large: 3½"

sugar stripes Dress

This cheery striped sheet is not typically something I would buy during a thrift-shop trip. The sheet was fresh and clean, but after close inspection, I found two small holes in the fabric. The wide and narrow striping and the just-off-white background was unusual, however, and ultimately made the buy a no-brainer. (I was able to use the sheet fabric just fine—I simply cut out my skirt fabric on the section of the sheet where there were no holes.)

The fabric print reminds me of the red-and-white striped pinafores that candy stripers used to wear over their dresses in the '50s and '60s. The fabric brings sugary-sweet candy canes to mind too. I combined the sweet sheet with a smart, sexy collared tank top to bring the sugar level down a bit—but not too much. I think I found a nice balance of sweet and sassy here.

my fiber facts

Size: Women's Medium; 66" x 96"/twin size

Content: 95% cotton, 5% spandex (top);
100% cotton (sheet)

design diversions

- Cut out a few small, identical shapes or motifs from leftover tank-top fabric (such as squares, triangles, flowers, squiggly lines, or spirals) and sew them onto the front of the skirt in a random pattern

- Add a small square or round pocket to the skirt front

- Add three *vertical* strips of tank-top fabric to the center of the waistband; vertical strips will require much less fabric than the horizontal strips, and they might look pretty cool, too

- Use the leftover sheet fabric—which you will likely have a lot of—to embellish the front and collar of the tank top with shapes you like

- Embellish the bottom of the skirt with appliquéd motifs cut from the sheet fabric

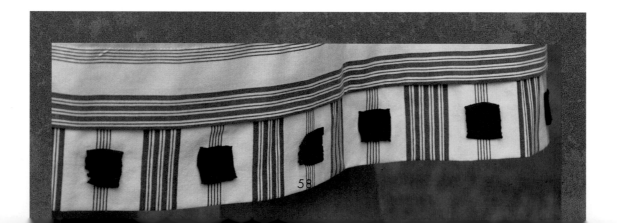

SUGAR STRIPES DRESS

GATHER YOUR MATERIALS

- One coordinating solid-colored, formfitting tank top in a *stretchy knit* fabric, with or without a collar*
- One twin-size print or striped flat sheet
- Thread to match tank-top fabric
- 3"-wide elastic to wrap loosely around your waist (found at most fabric stores)
- Safety pins, including one large safety pin (for inserting elastic)
- Dressmaker's measuring tape
- Rotary-cutting equipment (optional)
- Scissors
- Long straight edge, such as a ruler, book, or folder
- Fabric-marking tool
- Washable glue stick
- Long pins
- Large, flat object, such as a square rotary-cutting ruler, hardcover book, or baking sheet
- Seam ripper
- Hand sewing needle
- Freezer paper

Choose a longer top, rather than a shorter one, so you have more leftover fabric.

CUT AND SEW THE SKIRT, WAISTBAND, AND TANK TOP

1. Try on your formfitting tank top. To determine where the waistband should be, place your hands in the middle of your waist on either side, between the bottom of your ribs and your belly button (the place you might put your hands when you're growing impatient). This is where the center of your waistband should fall. Mark the waistband center with safety pins at the middle and sides of your tank top.

2. With the shirt still on, use a dressmaker's measuring tape to measure from the safety pin line to where you want your skirt hem to end. (Mine ends just above my knee.) Because the waistband will be about 3" wide, you'll need to subtract 1½" (half the waistband width) from the final length of your skirt.

Then subtract another 2" to account for the skirt border. Here's a simple formula to use. I've included my measurements to give you an example.

a. Measure from center of waist to just above the knee = ___" (mine is 25")

b. Subtract 3½" for waistband and skirt border= ___" (mine is 21½")

Note: If you're using a fitted sheet, add an extra 4" to make a 2"-wide doubled hem.

3. Use scissors or rotary-cutting equipment to cut away the side and bottom hemmed edges and selvages from the sheet; keep the top hem intact. Measure from the top hem to the length determined in step 2; cut across the width of the sheet. The cut edge will become the waist of your skirt and the top hem of the sheet will be the skirt hem. **1**

4. To make the waistband, we first need to measure your bust. This dress will come on and off over your head, and the waistband must be able to stretch over the widest part of your upper body. So, measure around the widest part of your bust. (Mine is 34½".) Add ½" to this measurement for seam allowances. From the remaining sheet fabric, cut two strips that measure 4¼" x your final bust measurement. (For me, the strips are 4¼" x 35".)

Note: If you're using stripes or a directional print, pay attention here. Cut the waistband so the stripe or print will be the opposite direction of the skirt fabric.

5. Lay the tank top right side out and right side up on a flat surface. Using a long straight edge as a guide, measure 1¼" above the safety pins placed

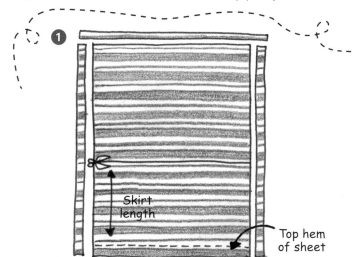

Skirt length

Top hem of sheet

in step 1; mark dots at this measurement along the front of the tank top. Make extra-dark dots on each side seam. Turn the tank top over; align your straight edge on the dots at the side seams and mark dots across the back of the tank top. Remove the safety pins and cut the tank top along the dotted lines with scissors, going through just one layer at a time for more accuracy. **2**

6. Cut 1½"-wide strips from the remaining tank top fabric for the waistband; keep the side seams intact as needed to get your length. Sew the short edges of the strips together and trim as needed to make a strip the same length as your final bust/waistband measurement from step 4. **3**

7. Place the pieced tank-top strip on the right side of one waistband strip from step 4, centering the tank-top strip from top to bottom; press in place with dots of glue stick. Sew ¼" away from each long edge of the tank-top strip, leaving the raw edges of the fabric exposed. **4**

   Note: If you're having trouble with sewing on the stretchy tank-top fabric, try feeding any stretch through gently by lifting your presser foot and nudging the fabric forward with your fingers every few inches. Pressing your right index finger next to the presser foot as you sew will also help with any stretching. But even if you do end up sewing in a few folds here and there, I promise that the gathering of the waistband later will forgive all.

RETIP *simple centering*

When centering the tank-top strip on the waistband, it's perfectly fine to "eyeball" the center. The fabric will be gathered later, which will crimp and curve both fabrics, hiding any small flaws.

8. With right sides together, sew the two long sides of the waistband strips together, forming a tube. Turn the tube right side out. Lay the tube on a flat surface and roll the seams outward and inward—with your fingers, as if you're using a rolling pin—until they lie flat; press.

9. To create a casing that will hold the waistband elastic inside, fold the waistband so the two *short* edges on the *front* of the waistband are touching. Align the raw edges and hold the two front layers together. Pin together so that the tank-top seams align. Then bump the waistband seams on both sides so they match up; pin. **5**

10. The sewing will be a little awkward, but take your time and stop often to adjust the position of the waistband as you sew. Beginning about ¼" from the bottom seam on the *wrong* side of the waistband, backstitch and then sew the two layers together using a ¼" seam allowance. Remove the

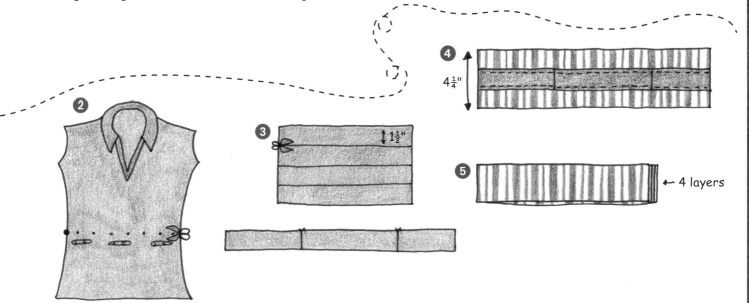

pins as you reach them, just before sewing. Sew the two *right* side waistband layers together, removing pins as you near the approaching seams; keep the seams aligned and sew about ¼" beyond them to the wrong side; backstitch for added strength. Now you have a reinforced opening to insert the elastic into later. 6

11. Try on the waistband. You should be able to pull it over your head and bust; it should fit loosely around your waist.

ATTACH TANK TOP TO WAISTBAND

1. Use pins to divide and mark the waistband into four equal parts. First, place one pin in the joining seam; this is a side seam. Lay the waistband flat and place a pin in the opposite edge. Now, refold the waistband so the two pins match in the center and lay it flat again. Place a pin at each new side fold. 7

2. Repeat step 1 to divide the bottom edge of the tank top into four equal parts, using the side seams as the first two placeholders. 8

3. Measure ½" above the bottom edge of the tank top and mark dots all the way around. Align a side-seam pin on the tank top with the side seam pin on the waistband; then align the top edge of

the waistband with the ½" dots on the tank top and pin. Pin the waistband on *top* of the tank top. Match up the other three pins on the waistband and tank top and pin those points in place, aligning the top of the waistband with the ½" dots.

4. Slide a large, flat object between the front and back layers of the tank top and waistband to prevent pinning the layers together. Working between one pair of pins at a time, pin the waistband all the way around the tank top, stretching the tank top as needed. Expect a lot of stretching—just keep stretching the tank top between each set of pins until it fits the waistband. 9

5. Starting at a side seam, sew the waistband to the tank top, stitching ¼" from the top of the waistband.

GATHER AND ATTACH THE SKIRT

1. Set your sewing machine to the longest stitch length. Sew ¼" from the raw edge across the top edge of the skirt fabric, leaving thread tails 6" to 8" long. Do *not* backstitch at the beginning or end of your stitching. Sew another row of stitching in the same manner, ¼" below the first. 10

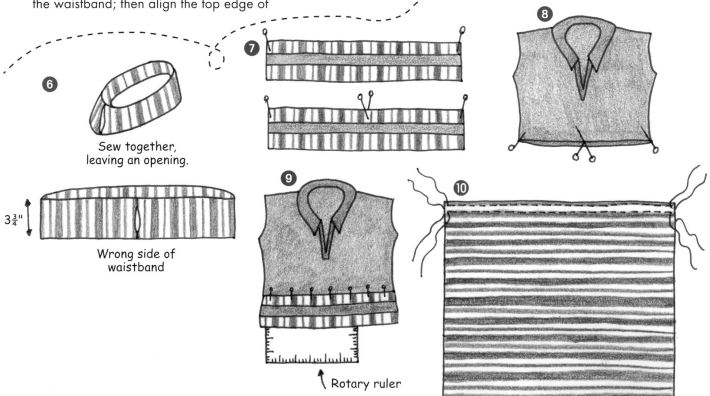

Sew together, leaving an opening.

$3\frac{3}{4}$"

Wrong side of waistband

Rotary ruler

2. Measure the full length of the waistband; divide by two and subtract ¼" from this measurement.

3. Find the center of your skirt by folding the skirt in half and marking the fold with a pin. To gather the skirt fabric, gently pull the bobbin threads on the two rows of stitching while gently pushing the fabric along toward the center pin. (The goal is to avoid breaking the thread—but you have a second row of stitching as backup, if you need it!) Gather the fabric until it matches the measurement from step 2. Tie the bobbin threads together so the gathers stay put. (I put the gathering thread ends onto a needle and take a few stitches for reinforcement.) Repeat to gather the other side of the skirt. **11**

4. Fold the skirt in half with right sides together; match up the lengthwise raw edges and pin. Using a ¼" seam allowance, sew the skirt into a tube. (Don't forget to reset your stitch length!) Press the seam allowances open.

5. Just as you did when attaching the waistband to the tank top, divide the bottom of the waistband and the top of the skirt into four equal parts. Align the bottom edge of the waistband with the ½" gathering seam on the skirt, using that seam as a guide as you pin all the way around. Slide a large,

flat object between the front and back of the skirt and waistband layers to prevent pinning layers together. Pin the waistband on *top* of the skirt, and make sure the skirt seam aligns with the waistband seam. Work in sections between the pins, easing the skirt fabric to fit the waistband as necessary. **12**

6. Beginning at the side seam, stitch along the waistband, ¼" from the pinned edge, to sew the waistband to the skirt. After sewing, use a seam ripper to carefully remove any gathering stitches that show on the outside of the dress.

7. Wrap the 3"-wide elastic around the middle of your waist (you'll want a snug fit). Add 1" and cut the elastic to this measurement. Turn the dress wrong side out and follow the instructions for "Inserting Elastic" (page 33) to gather the waistband. After sewing the ends of the elastic together, whipstitch the opening closed. Distribute gathers evenly. **13** **14**

MAKE AND ATTACH THE SKIRT BORDER

If you used a fitted sheet and have a raw edge at the bottom of your skirt, now is the time to turn it under 2" and sew a hem.

1. Determine the length to cut strips for the skirt border by laying the skirt tube flat, folded at the seam. Smooth out the front and back layers and measure across the bottom hem. Multiply this measurement by 2; add ½" for seams.

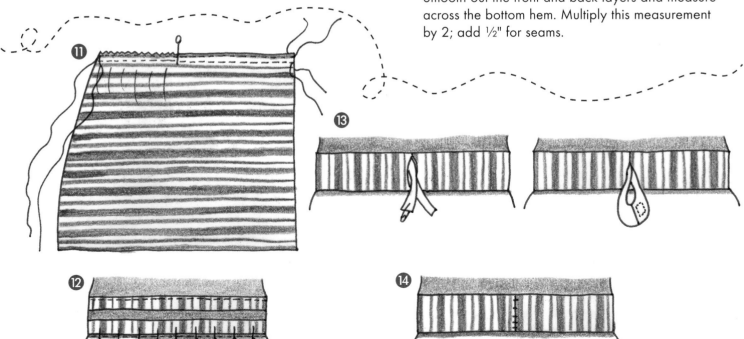

2. To determine the *width* to cut the skirt border strip, measure the width of the sheet hem. Multiply that measurement by 4 and add ½" for seams. This is your final strip width. (If you added a 2" hem yourself, the width of your strip would be 8½".)

3. From the remaining sheet fabric, cut a strip to the measurements determined in steps 1 and 2. You may need to piece the short edges of two or three strips together to achieve the length needed. If you're using striped or directional fabric, cut the strips so the pattern is going in the opposite direction of the skirt.

4. With right sides together and using a ¼" seam allowance, sew the two short edges of the strip together to form a tube; press the seam allowances open. With *wrong* sides together, fold the strip in half lengthwise and press. ⑮

5. To sew the border to the skirt, turn the skirt inside out. Lay the border tube so it overlaps the bottom of the skirt hem by ¼". Match up the skirt side seam with the border seam; pin the seams together. Slide a large rotary-cutting ruler or similar object between the front and back layers of the skirt and the border and pin around the entire skirt. Sew the border to the skirt, stitching ¼" from the raw edges of the border. ⑯

6. The appliquéd squares are 1" x 1" and spaced evenly around the hem at 1½" intervals. To determine how many squares to cut from the tank-top fabric, divide the final strip length from step 1 by 2½". (I encourage you to use the patterns in the fabric as a guide. I used the stripes in my fabric to determine where to place each square.)

7. Turn the skirt right side out and lay it flat. Place the squares evenly around the border at 1½" intervals, centering the squares from top to bottom and pressing each square in place with a dot of glue stick. Sew around each square ¼" from the edges, leaving the raw edges exposed. ⑰

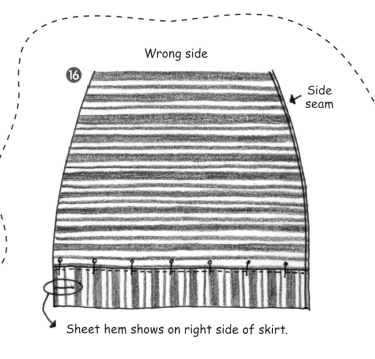

Wrong side

Side seam

⑯

Sheet hem shows on right side of skirt.

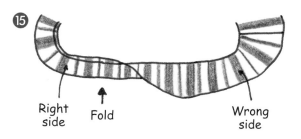

⑮

Right side   Fold   Wrong side

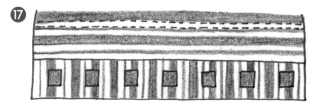

⑰

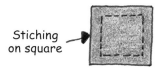

Stiching on square

MAKE AND ATTACH
THE OPTIONAL COLLAR

Your tank top may or may not have a collar; if it does, follow these instructions to add the collar embellishment using the sheet fabric.

1. Lay out a length of freezer paper on a flat surface, shiny side down. Place the collar of the tank top on the freezer paper; smooth it out to lie flat. Trace around one short edge, the long back edge, and the opposite short edge of the collar. Remove the tank top and draw a line to connect the bottom of the short ends together. On the two short sides, cut out the collar shape on the drawn lines. On the two long sides, cut the collar shape ¼" outside the drawn lines to complete the template. **18**

2. Fold a length of sheet fabric in half right sides together, making sure it is big enough for the entire collar made from freezer paper. Also note the orientation of stripes or directional print so that you cut the collar with the print or stripe running as desired. Press the fold of the sheet fabric. Place the collar template on the fabric, shiny side down, and press in place (the paper will temporarily stick to the fabric). Carefully cut through both layers of fabric around the template, ¼" outside all of the drawn lines.

3. Remove the freezer paper and sew around one short edge, the long back edge, and the opposite short edge of the collar using a ¼" seam allowance. Leave the edge closest to the neck open. Turn the collar right side out and press; press under a ¼" seam allowance along the open edge of the collar. **19**

4. Find the centers of the tank collar and the sheet collar by folding both in half and inserting a pin at each midpoint. Lay the tank collar flat, back side up; lay the sheet collar on top of the tank collar, aligning the folded and pressed edge of the sheet collar with the seam that connects the collar to the tank top. (The folded-under edges of the sheet collar should lie against the tank collar.) Match up the center pins of both collars; then pin the collars together, bumping the folded edge of the sheet collar against the seam that connects the collar to the tank top. Using thread that matches the tank top, sew ⅛" away from folded-under edges, along the seam that connects the collar to the tank top. **20**

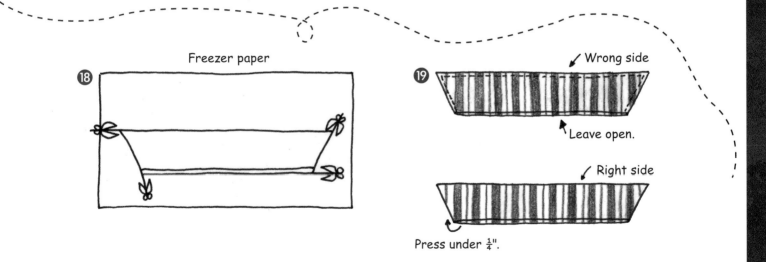

Freezer paper

18

19 Wrong side

Leave open.

Right side

Press under ¼".

20

Back collar view

diner DRESS

I made this dress, reminiscent of those worn by diner waitresses, four times before I decided which one I liked best. There are so many wonderful button-down shirts at the thrift store—in both the men's and the women's sections—and I wanted to take advantage of all the fun, funky colors and patterns. You'll be surprised at the rainbow of colors available in casual and dress shirts alike. (Dress number three was made from pink and purple shirts, all men's.) If you like the buttonhole waistband on this dress, you'll want to make sure that at least two of the men's shirts you use come with a "cut-and-keep" buttonhole panel; refer to "Cut the Shirts" step 6 (page 68) for details.

my fiber facts

Size: Men's Large (3 shirts); Women's Medium (fitted shirt)

Content: 100% cotton (men's shirts); 94% cotton, 6% spandex (fitted shirt)

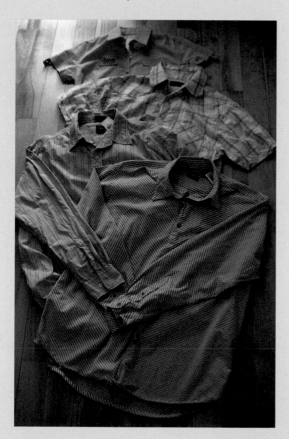

design diversions

- Make your dress with a long-sleeve fitted blouse
- Cut the sleeves shorter if your perfect fitted shirt has long sleeves
- Make a sleeveless dress by removing sleeves entirely
- Add patch pockets to the skirt using leftover shirt fabric or a different coordinating fabric

GATHER YOUR MATERIALS

- 3 men's button-down shirts in coordinating colors/prints (the larger the width, the fuller the skirt)*
- 1 women's fitted button-down shirt** in a color that coordinates with the men's shirts
- Thread to match shirts and shirt buttons
- Scissors
- Rotary-cutting equipment (optional, but very helpful)
- Long pins
- Safety pins
- A long straight edge, such as a ruler or book
- Fabric-marking tool
- Hand-sewing needle
- Seam ripper
- Dressmaker's measuring tape

*Include at least one shirt with long sleeves if you plan to make a waistband instead of using buttonhole panels.

**This shirt is for the dress bodice and should fit your form snugly.

DINER DRESS

CUT THE SHIRTS

1. Lay one of the men's shirts flat, right side out and right side up. Button up all buttons and flip the collar up. Use scissors to cut out the entire front of the shirt—up the side seams, up the armholes to the shoulder, across the shoulder seams, and around the neckline, removing all seams. ❶

2. Cut the back of the shirt in the same manner—cut away the side seams, cut up the armholes to the shoulder seam, and then cut across the shoulder seams and neckline (include the shoulder panel across the back of the shirt, if there is one). Again, remove all seams. ❷

3. Repeat steps 1 and 2 to cut the other two men's shirts.

4. Decide which men's shirt you would like to button up the front of the skirt. We'll call this shirt A. Cut the widest rectangle you can from the front of shirt A; do not cut away any of the length. A rotary cutter, ruler, and mat are great for this step, but scissors will work too. ❸

5. Cut the widest rectangle you can from the back of shirt A, and then cut it in half lengthwise. ❹

6. Decide which shirt you would like to attach to either side of shirt A at the front of the skirt. We'll call this shirt B. The third shirt we'll call shirt C. Examine the buttonhole panels (also known as *plackets*) for shirts B and C. They should look like one of these shown. ❺

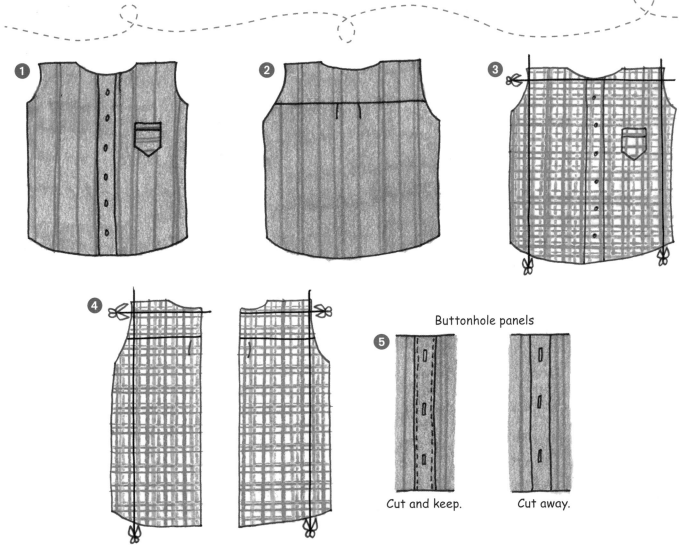

Buttonhole panels

Cut and keep.   Cut away.

7. If your B or C shirt fronts have a "cut-and-keep" *buttonhole* panel, slide your scissors underneath the finished edge of the placket and carefully cut it away from the shirt, keeping the long folded edge of the placket intact. Save the plackets for later. If your shirt fronts have "cut-away" buttonhole plackets, carefully cut them away from the shirt and discard (or keep for another project). Then, carefully cut away the *button* edge on both shirt fronts, keeping as much of the shirt fabric intact as you can. ❻

   Note: You'll need two cut-and-keep buttonhole plackets for the skirt waistband. If you have just one cut-and-keep panel—or none—don't fret! I've provided alternate directions for turning long sleeves from one of your shirts into a waistband.

8. Cut the widest rectangles you can from the fronts of shirts B and C (for a total of four panels). Do not cut away any of the length.

RETIP *plan for pleats*

If you come across a pleat on any of the shirt backs (most likely, you will), it's easy to incorporate it into your design. Fold and pin both sides of the pleat in place all the way down the length of the shirt. Make sure your pins point toward the top or bottom of the shirt instead of from side to side. Leave the pins in place until you have made your skirt into a tube; then remove the pins.

9. Cut the back of shirt in half lengthwise; cut the halves into the widest rectangles you can as you did before. Do not cut away any of the length. Leave the back of shirt C as one piece; cut it into the widest rectangle you can. ❼

10. Try on the women's button-down shirt. Place your hands in the middle of your waist on either side, between the bottom of your ribs and your belly button (the place you might put your hands when you are growing impatient). This is where the center of your waistband should fall. Mark the waistband center with safety pins at the middle and sides of the shirt. ❽

Buttonhole panels

Cut and keep.   Cut away.

Button panels

Cut away.

Shirt back (B)

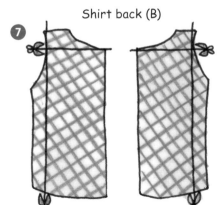

Shirt back (C)

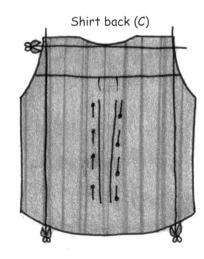

DINER DRESS

11. Lay the shirt right side out and right side up on a flat surface. Using a long straight edge as a guide, measure ¼" above the safety pins placed in step 10; mark dots at this measurement along the front of the shirt. Make darker dots on each side seam. Turn the shirt over; align your straight edge on the dots at the side seams and mark dots across the back of the shirt. Remove the safety pins and use scissors to cut the shirt along the dotted lines, going through just one layer at a time for more accuracy. **9**

Note: If your line runs into a button and buttonhole, shift your entire cutting line ¼" above or below—whichever is closer to your original markings. You can adjust the placement of the waistband later to compensate for the move.

MAKE AND ATTACH THE SKIRT

1. Lay the front and back pieces of shirts A, B, and C next to each other as shown. **10**

2. Starting at one end, pin two adjacent pieces right sides together with the top edges aligned. Sew from the top edge to the bottom of the shorter piece using a ¼" seam allowance. Continue until all the pieces are joined; then join front-piece B and back-piece C to form a tube. Press the seam allowances open. Unbutton the front of shirt A so your skirt tube becomes one flat piece again.

3. Set your sewing machine to the longest stitch length. Starting just beyond the buttonhole placket, sew ¼" from the top raw edge until you reach the hem at the button edge. Leave thread tails 6" to 8" long; do *not* backstitch at the beginning or end of your stitching. Sew another row of stitching in the same manner, ¼" below the first.

4. Find the center back of the skirt by folding the skirt in half widthwise and marking the fold with a pin. Unbutton the women's button-down shirt. Find the center back of the shirt by folding the bottom of the shirt in half widthwise and marking the fold with a pin. Place the shirt right side up on a flat surface, so the back of the shirt faces you and the collar is closer to your body than the bottom edge. Smooth out the bottom of the shirt so it lies flat.

5. Gather the skirt by gently pulling the bobbin threads on the two rows of stitching while gently pushing the fabric along the thread toward the center pin. (The goal is to avoid breaking the thread—but you have a second row of stitching as backup, if you need it!) Gather the fabric until it approximately matches the width of *one half* of the

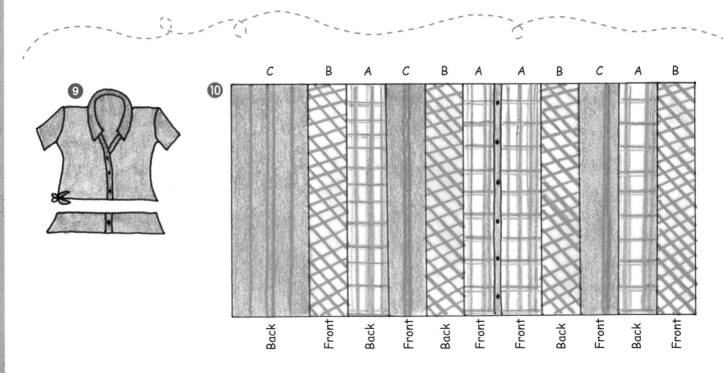

bottom of the shirt (from the edge of the buttonhole panel to the center pin). Repeat to gather the other side of the skirt. ⑪

6. Place the gathered skirt on top of the shirt, right sides together, and align the edges. Pin the pieces together at the center pin. Now, gather or loosen the skirt until it matches the width of one half of the shirt exactly. Tie the bobbin threads together so the gathers stay put. (I put the gathering thread ends onto a needle and take a few stitches for reinforcement.) Pin the outside edges of the shirt and skirt together; then pin between the edge and center pin, easing the skirt as needed. Repeat on the other side. ⑫

7. Using a ¼" machine *basting* stitch (the longest stitch length on your sewing machine), sew the skirt to the shirt. Make sure the gathers are on the top so you can see them as you sew and nudge the gathers straight as needed before they pass under the needle. Press the seam allowances toward the shirt. Inspect the seam on the right side to make sure all gathers are sewn in and no adjustments are needed; then sew over your basting stitches using a normal stitch length. After sewing, use a seam ripper to carefully remove any gathering/basting stitches that show on the outside of the dress.

MOVE THE BUTTONS (MAYBE…)

You probably know that men's shirts and women's shirts button on opposite sides. So when you try on your dress at this point, you may run into a problem—the shirt buttons up in one direction and the skirt buttons up in the other direction. If your shirt and skirt button up in the same direction, great—you can move on to the next section. If they don't (mine, to my shock, didn't!), there's a fairly quick fix—we'll simply reverse the placement of the buttons on the button edge of the skirt. Here's what to do.

Note: The shirt that I used for the front of my skirt had a solid blue button panel that added a nice contrast to the front of the dress. The blue fabric was part of the original shirt.

1. Carefully remove the buttons from shirt A (now your skirt front) with a seam ripper. Count how many buttons you removed. Remove the same number of buttons from shirt B or C. Choose the button you like best for the *right* side of panel A; use the other buttons for the *wrong* side of panel A.

2. Thread a hand-sewing needle with thread that coordinates with the buttons that will show on the front. Use a doubled length of thread and knot the end. Poke your needle from the wrong side of the button panel to the right side, following the

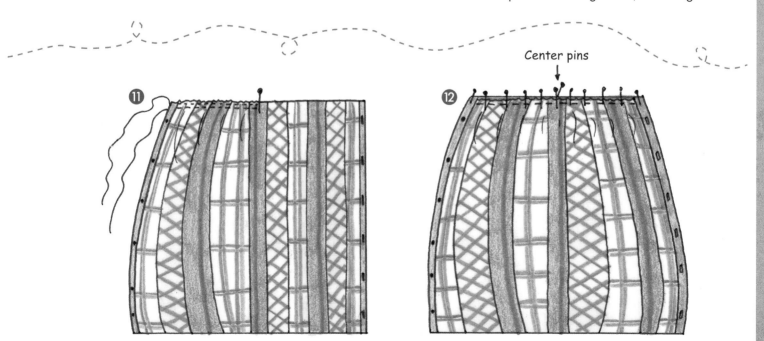

Center pins

DINER DRESS

small holes that the previous button left behind. Thread a favorite button onto the *right* side of the panel (the side that will show on the front); poke your needle back through the button to secure it in place and pull the needle to the wrong side of the button panel. Now, thread the other button onto the needle so it is on the *wrong* side of the button panel; poke your needle back through to the front, going through another hole of the button on the right side. Be sure not to pull the thread too tightly; keep it a bit loose so the buttons have a little wiggle room—basically, enough wiggle that you can get another layer of fabric between them. **13**

3. Continue sewing the two buttons to each other until they are secure; then knot the thread on the *wrong* side of the button panel, underneath the button. Clip the thread close to the knot; then nudge the knot under the button with a seam ripper or long pin to hide it. Repeat this step with the remaining buttons.

4. When you button your skirt, you'll use the button on the *wrong* side of the button panel. The button on the *right* side of the button panel is decorative only. (Sneaky, huh?)

CUT AND SEW THE WAISTBAND

There are two options for sewing a waistband. You can use the buttonhole plackets from shirts B and C or you can use strips from a long sleeve from shirts A, B, or C.

Use Buttonhole Plackets

1. Choose your favorite buttonhole placket to use as a waistband on the front of the dress. We'll cut this placket into two pieces, one for each side of the front of the dress.

2. Starting with the side of the dress that has buttons, measure from the shirt side seam to the edge of the button panel. Add 2¾" to this measurement. Cut the waistband to this measurement, starting your cut 2½" from the edge of one buttonhole (this will become a functioning buttonhole). **14**

3. Fold the edge with the functioning buttonhole toward the wrong side of the panel ¼" and press. Fold under another ¼" and press. Hold the folds in place with pins. **15**

4. Now measure from the other shirt side seam to the edge of the buttonhole panel. Add 1½" to this measurement and cut a waistband piece for this side of the dress. Fold one short edge of this waistband piece ¼" toward the wrong side and press. Hold the fold in place with pins. **16**

5. Finally, choose the buttonhole placket you would like to sew to the back of the dress. Measure from side seam to side seam along the back of the shirt; add ½" to this measurement. Cut the buttonhole placket to this measurement, centering buttonholes as you would like them to show on the back of the dress.

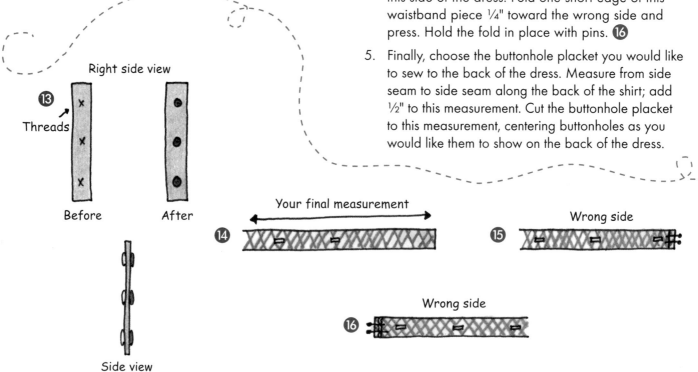

Right side view

13 Threads

Before   After

Side view

Your final measurement

14

Wrong side

15

Wrong side

16

6. Lay out the three waistband pieces side by side, making sure the front waistband pieces are on the correct sides of the back waistband. With right sides together and using a ¼" seam allowance, sew the end of each front piece to the ends of the back piece. Press the seam allowances open and clip the corners of the seam allowances inward diagonally, close to the stitching. ⓱

7. Unbutton the dress and lay it flat, right side up. Center the waistband along the seam that joins the shirt and skirt, matching the side seams of the waistband and shirt and easing as needed. If you cut your shirt a little shorter or longer to avoid a buttonhole, adjust the placement of your waistband down or up accordingly. Secure with a few pins, try on the dress, and adjust the waistline placement as needed. Fold in the shorter end of the waistband 1" to the wrong side and pin. Pin the top edge of the waistband all the way around the back of the dress and to the other side of the front of the dress. You should have a 2" waistband overhang on the button side of the skirt. ⓲

8. Starting at the bottom of the waistband on the buttonhole side of the skirt, sew along the short edge of the waistband ⅛" from the edge. Turn at the corner of the waistband and sew all the way around the top of the waistband ⅛" from the edge, removing pins as you go. When you reach the end of the button side of the skirt, sew down the short overhang edge. Backstitch, remove the dress from the machine, and pin the bottom edge of the waistband all the way around the dress. ⓳

9. Starting where you left off on the button side of the skirt, sew along the bottom edge of the waistband to the buttonhole side, removing pins as you go. ⓴

10. Try on the dress and button it up. Pull the overhang of the waistband snugly against the dress to determine where to sew on a button. Use a marking tool to make a dot inside the functioning buttonhole, so the dot shows up on the waistband. Remove the dress and sew a button at the dot.

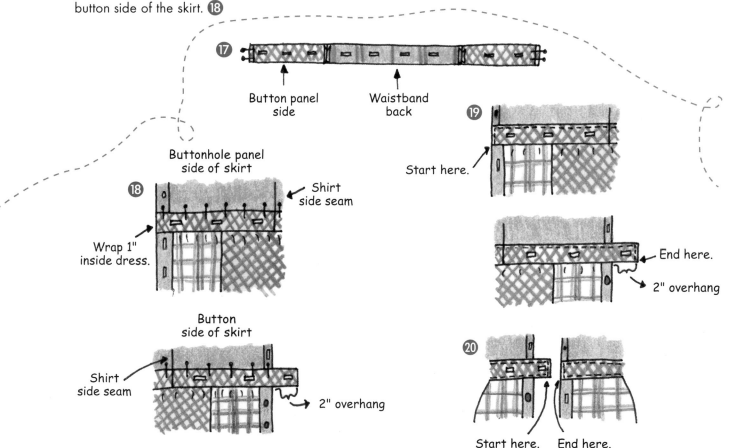

⓱

Button panel side   Waistband back

Buttonhole panel side of skirt

⓲   Shirt side seam

Wrap 1" inside dress.

⓳   Start here.

End here.

2" overhang

Button side of skirt

Shirt side seam

2" overhang

⓴

Start here.   End here.

Use a Long Sleeve

1. Unbutton the dress and lay it on a flat surface, right side up. Measure from one edge of the dress to the other, across the shirt/skirt seam. Add 3½" to this measurement.

2. Choose a long sleeve from shirt A, B, or C to use as the waistband. Cut along the seam of the sleeve; cut away the cuff. Lay the sleeve on a flat surface. Beginning at the middle of the sleeve (where the longest strips can be cut), cut strips that measure 2¾" wide. Cut as many strips from the sleeve as you need to achieve your waistband measurement from step 1 plus a few extra inches. Use the second sleeve, if needed.

3. Sew the short edges of the strips together using a ¼" seam allowance; press the seam allowances open. Cut the pieced strip to your final waistband measurement from step 1. Fold the strip lengthwise, *wrong* sides together, and pin. Sew the long edges of the strip together using a ¼" seam allowance so you have a tube. Roll the seam allowance to the center of the tube; press the seam allowances open. The side without the seam in the center is now the front of your waistband. **21**

RETIP *multi-fabric waistband*

If you want your waistband to showcase more than one fabric, you can use shorter lengths of fabric from different sleeves. Just remember to allow ½" extra for every seam you create and keep your final waistband measurement exact.

4. Determine which side of your waistband will end on the buttonhole side of the skirt. Fold the short edge of this side of the waistband ¼" toward the wrong side and press. Fold under another ¼" and press. Hold the folds in place with pins.

5. Make a buttonhole ½" from the edge. Follow the instructions in your sewing machine manual, use your own technique, or use the technique in "Newsboy Cap and Scarf Set" (page 110, step 7). **22**

6. Fold the short edge on the opposite side of the waistband ¼" toward the wrong side; press and pin to hold the fold in place.

7. Follow steps 7–10 of "Use Buttonhole Plackets" (page 73) to attach the waistband to the dress and add a button.

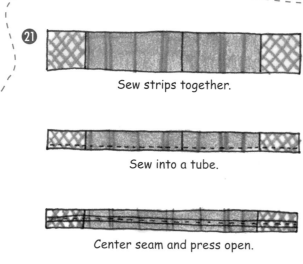

21 Sew strips together.

Sew into a tube.

Center seam and press open.

22 $\frac{1}{2}$"

HEM THE DRESS

1. Unbutton the dress and lay it on a flat surface, spreading out the skirt so the bottom edge lies flat. Find the shortest shirt piece at the bottom of the skirt. Cut each shirt piece so it is the same length as the shortest one. Starting at one edge, cut across one shirt piece at a time. Use the skirt seams as a guide—making sure your cuts are perpendicular to the skirt seams—to cut a straight hem across the bottom of the skirt. Rotary-cutting equipment is very helpful for this step, but careful cutting with scissors will also do the trick. Be sure you cut away all seaming and hems, including the shortest shirt piece. **23**

2. Try on the dress. With a ¼" hem, the skirt will shrink up by ½". If you want a shorter skirt, determine how many inches shorter and divide that number in half to determine the hem fold measurement. Turn the bottom edge of the skirt ¼" or the hem fold measurement to the *wrong* side; press. Turn again by the same measurement and press again. Pin the hem in place to hold the fold. Stitch next to the folded edge with the *wrong* side of the dress facing up on your sewing machine (so you can make sure you are catching the hem all the way around). **24**

RETIP *the finishing touches*

There was a funny little beach-resort logo on my women's button-down shirt. I wanted to hide it so I created a raw-edge appliqué detail using rectangles cut from the leftover men's shirt fabrics. I dotted the rectangles with glue stick, pressed them down where I wanted them on the shirt, and then sewed ¼" from the raw edges all around the rectangles. My rectangles, from large to small, measured 2¼" x 3", 1¾" x 2½", and 1¼" x 2". If you like your dress as is, then you're done! Cut and appliqué rectangles if you would like to duplicate the detail I made on the shirt, or make a detail that is entirely your own.

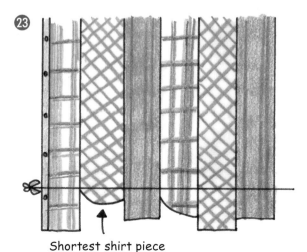

Shortest shirt piece

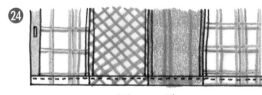

Wrong side

shirred sheet DRESS

I thrifted this sheet for no other reason than that I loved the crisp colors. After getting my treasure home, I decided to create a simple summer dress that was long and lean. I knew I wanted buttons, but I didn't want to sew my own buttonholes. That's where men's dress shirts came in!

I guess it would take about the same amount of time to harvest buttons and buttonholes from the shirts as it would to sew your own "from scratch." But I think the shirt pieces give the dress a fresh, unique look.

my fiber facts

Size: 66" x 96"/twin size; Men's 16–36; Men's 15½–33

Content: 100% cotton (sheet and one shirt); 65% polyester, 35% cotton (shirt)

design diversions

- Cut the length of the skirt to where your button/buttonhole panels end
- Skip the waistband so you can skip a step
- Go strapless! (and skip another step)
- Make straps from leftover shirt fabrics instead of sheet fabric
- Make the waistband from leftover shirt fabrics instead of sheet fabric

GATHER YOUR MATERIALS

- One twin-size flat sheet
- Two button-down men's dress shirts in colors that coordinate with sheet
- Thread to coordinate with sheet fabric
- Elastic thread (available in white and black at most fabric stores; look where elastic is displayed)
- Dressmaker's measuring tape
- Scissors
- Rotary-cutting equipment (optional, but helpful)
- Piece of scrap fabric, at least 6" x 12", for shirring practice
- Spray bottle of water
- Long pins
- Washable glue stick
- Safety pin
- Fabric-marking tool

CUT THE SHEET

1. Determine the length to cut your dress by placing the start of a dressmaker's measuring tape where you want your dress to start (I placed mine under my arm); then let the tape fall to the floor. Take the measurement just above your ankle or wherever you want your dress hem to end. Call this measurement A. (My measurement was 50".)

SHIRRED SHEET DRESS

2. To determine the width of fabric for your dress, measure around your bust and multiply by 1½. Subtract 2" (for the button and buttonhole plackets) to get your final width measurement, which we'll call B. (My bust measurement was 34". Multiply: 34" x 1½ = 51". Subtract: 51" – 2" = 49". My final measurement was 49".)

3. Use scissors or rotary-cutting equipment to cut away one side seam or selvage from the sheet. Treating the top hem of the sheet as a hem for the *bottom* of your dress, cut the sheet lengthwise to measurement A and widthwise from the cut edge to measurement B. ●

4. Sew along the top raw edge of the dress fabric using a tight zigzag stitch.

SHIRR THE FABRIC

If you've never tried shirring before, there's no need to tense up—after you get the hang of it, it's like sewing magic! Just be sure to experiment on a scrap of fabric to get the feel of shirring before you sew on your dress fabric.

1. First prepare your sewing machine with a few tweaks. Start by *hand winding* the elastic thread onto an empty bobbin. Do *not* pull the thread tightly as you wind; just give it enough tension to stay on the bobbin.

2. Insert the bobbin into your machine and thread your machine as you normally do, using regular sewing thread in the needle. If you have trouble getting the elastic thread to pull from the bobbin case, loosen your bobbin tension.

3. Set your machine to a long stitch length (I used not-quite machine basting length, but close). Position your scrap fabric to sew along the length. Begin sewing ¼" from one short edge and about ½" from the long edge of your scrap fabric. Take a couple of stitches and backstitch; sew forward a couple stitches and backstitch again so that your stitches are securely anchored. Sew forward and you'll notice the fabric starting to gather on its own behind the needle. When you reach the end of the fabric, repeat the anchoring backstitch and clip the threads.

4. Begin a second row about ¼" from the first row and sew in the same manner. I used the right edge of my presser foot, which is about ¼", as a guide from row to row. If you are new to shirring, I suggest completing about 10 rows on your scrap fabric before moving on to your dress.

RETIP *shirring success*

As you keep adding rows, the fabric gathers more and more. To keep fabric straight and flat, try these tips:

• Place the palm of your left hand flat on the ungathered fabric and let it guide the fabric on the left side of the needle.

• Use your right hand to tug the fabric gently toward your body, which will also help flatten the gathers before the fabric goes under the needle. This hand can help guide the fabric as well.

5. To shirr the bodice of the dress, begin your first row ¼" from the zigzag stitching at the top edge. Be sure to backstitch well at the beginning and end of every row to ensure that your stitches are well anchored and don't come loose later. Shirr across the entire width of the dress. Cut the threads and begin another row about ¼" away.

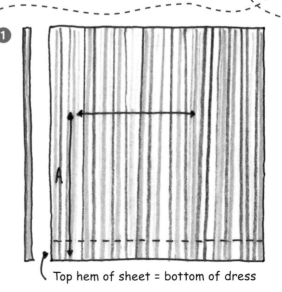

Top hem of sheet = bottom of dress

6. Continue in this manner until you have sewn 10 rows. Now, hold the dress to your chest and place the top edge where you want your dress to begin. The shirring should end at the bottom of your rib cage, so keep sewing rows and holding the dress up to your body until you have enough rows to cover your rib cage. (I sewed 29 rows.) **2**

7. When your shirring is completed, lay the dress on a flat surface and spray the shirred area with water so it will shrink further together. Allow to air-dry.

RETIP *bobbin alert*

With this many rows to shirr, you'll need to hand wind your bobbin with elastic thread several times. Before starting a new row of shirring, check to make sure you have enough elastic thread on the bobbin to complete the row you're sewing. All is not lost if you run out of elastic thread in the middle of a row, but it does compromise the staying power of your shirring over time. If you do run out of elastic thread in the middle of a row, you can either pick out the stitching and start again or you can knot the end of the elastic thread on the dress, and then backstitch over the last few stitches when you start sewing again.

CUT THE SHIRTS, MAKE THE BUTTON PLACKETS

1. Button up both dress shirts, flip up the collars, and lay them flat, right side up. Using scissors, cut a generous ¼" outside each buttonhole placket along the length of the shirt. Cut across each placket at the collar, leaving the top button that is attached to the collar behind. **3**

2. Your pieces, when unbuttoned, should look as shown. **4**

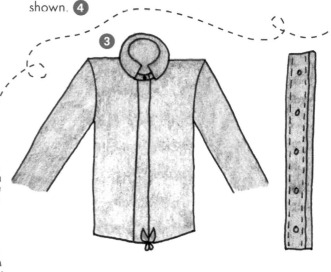

Generous ¼"

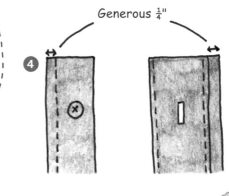

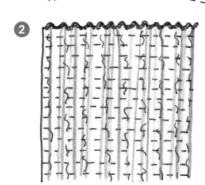

SHIRRED SHEET DRESS

3. Lay each button piece and buttonhole placket, still buttoned together, on a flat surface. Measure between the buttonholes and cut across the width of the panels at the halfway point between each. The button/buttonhole units from each shirt should measure exactly the same length. **5**

4. Unbutton the units and lay the matching pieces side by side, alternating pairs from shirt to shirt and taking care to keep track of the pairs. (The *finished* edges should always be on the same side from unit to unit.)

5. Alternating between button/buttonhole units of the two shirts, place right sides together. With the finished edges aligned and using an as-accurate-as-you-can 1/4" seam allowance, sew the short edges of the buttonhole pieces together. Then, sew the short edges of the button pieces together in the same manner. Use all of the button/buttonhole units you have from each shirt; as shown in the photo (page 77), the total length of your sewn units will not be as long as your dress. Press the button/buttonhole units with the seam allowances open. **6**

6. Button up the resewn placket; if your sewing was accurate, the buttons will match the buttonholes. If there are any buttons that don't quite match up with the buttonholes, you can take in or let out the first seams you sewed by a small amount to make adjustments. To take in a seam, simply sew using a slightly wider seam allowance. To let out a seam, sew using a narrower seam allowance, and then use your seam ripper to pick out the first line of stitching. Once you're satisfied with the matches, unbutton the placket.

7. Trim the seam allowances to 1/8"; press them open. **7**

RETIP *even on the edge*

Your button/buttonhole pieces may vary slightly in width; that's okay. Just make sure the *finished* edges of all the units are aligned; that is what will show on the dress. Any excess seam allowance on the other side of the units will be hidden on the inside of the dress.

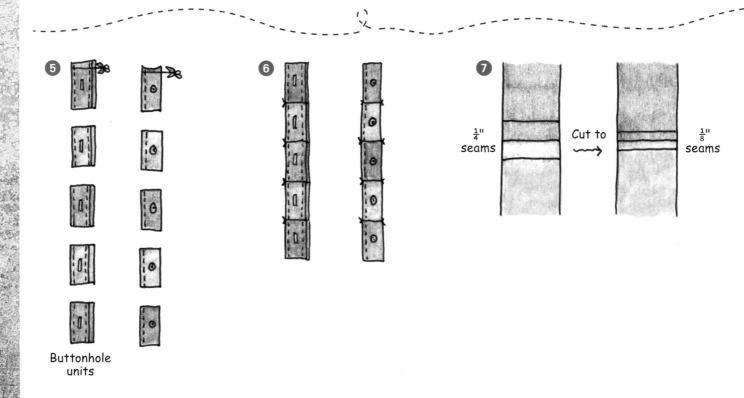

5 Buttonhole units

6

7 1/4" seams — Cut to → — 1/8" seams

8. Cut a long 1"-wide strip from the remaining sheet fabric; this will be used to cover the seams along the button and buttonhole plackets. Pay attention to any directional patterns and cut the strip so the pattern goes in your preferred direction. You'll need about 90", so you may need to cut more than one strip. Fold one long edge of the strip ¼" toward the wrong side of the fabric and press. Fold the other long edge ¼" toward the wrong side of the fabric and press. **8**

9. Use the glue stick to adhere the strip of fabric from step 8 to the seams across the width of the button/buttonhole plackets. Use a glue stick to dot glue on the right and wrong side of the first seam on the placket. Center one short edge of the strip on one seam, aligning the raw edges. Wrap the strip around to the back of the panel and finger-press it in place; the glue stick should hold both sides of the strip to the panel. Cut the strip so it is aligned with the raw edges. Sew just inside the folded edges of the strip on three sides (not on the raw edge side). **9**

10. Repeat step 9 on each seam of the buttonhole placket. Also enclose the raw edges at the top and bottom with the strips from step 8. Repeat to sew strips to the button placket seams and the top and bottom edges.

RETIP *button up*

To make sure your button and buttonhole plackets match up precisely, button the two plackets together. This will let you see how well the strips are matching up, and you can make minor adjustments up or down accordingly.

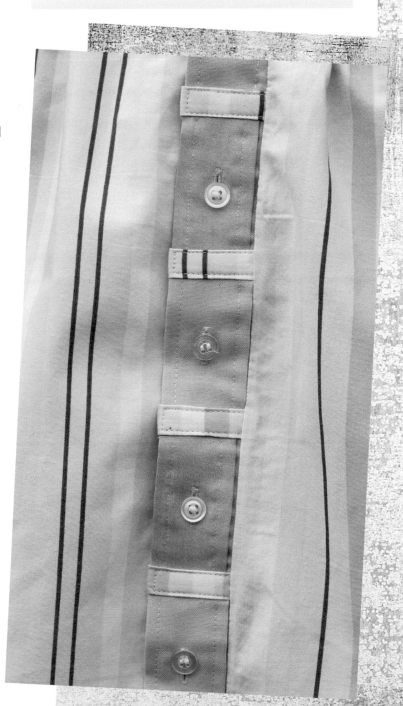

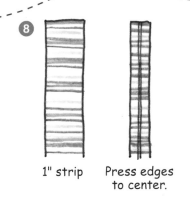

8

1" strip   Press edges to center.

9

Align raw edges.   Wrap and cut.   Sew.

MAKE THE WAISTBAND

1. With the dress open and lying flat, use a dress-maker's measuring tape to measure across the width of the dress along the *bottom* row of shirring. Add 5" to that measurement (for insurance). From the remaining sheet fabric, cut a 4½"-wide strip to that length.

2. With right sides together, sew the two long edges of the strip together to form a tube. Turn the tube inside out; press so that the seam is centered on one side of the tube. This is your waistband. **10**

3. Align one short end of the waistband tube with one edge of the dress; pin the tube to the dress so one long edge of the waistband follows the last shirred seam. Try not to stretch the shirring; just let it lie flat as you pin. Pull the gathers on the skirt portion of the dress straight and perpendicular to the waistband and pin well at the edges of the dress. There will be excess waistband fabric on the other edge of the dress; do not cut it away just yet. **11**

4. Align the buttonhole placket on the wearer's right side of the dress, right sides together. Starting ¼" from the top edge of the dress, pin and then machine *baste* the buttonhole placket to the dress using a ¼" seam allowance. Avoid sewing over the pins at the waistband edge. **12**

5. Repeat step 4 to machine baste the button placket to the other side of the dress. **13**

Note: Be careful when sewing past the buttons themselves—if you sew too quickly, they may move your fabric and you'll end up with wonky seams.

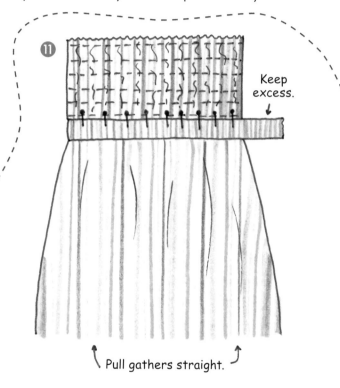

Keep excess.

Pull gathers straight.

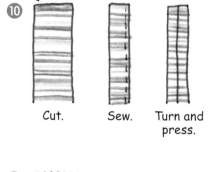

10 Cut. Sew. Turn and press.

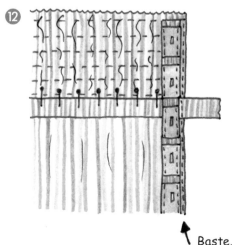

12 Baste.

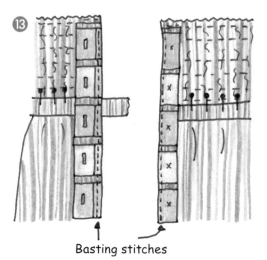

13 Basting stitches

As you approach each button, use the hand wheel on your machine to manually stitch past the button; stitch normally between the buttons.

6. Now is the time to carefully try on your dress (watch out for pins and try not to disturb the basting stitches—they are prone to unravel easily). Button up the dress and check the fit. Check for two things:

   • Do the buttons and buttonholes match up? If they do, great! If they don't, you may need to unpick your basting stitches in those spots where they don't. Ease and pin the panels so they line up more accurately. Then, rebaste the unpicked portion of the seam.

   • Does the waistband seem too loose or too tight? If it fits just right, great! If it seems loose, unpick the basting seam that holds the side of the waistband with the excess fabric (unpick the seam holding the waistband only; no need to unpick the entire seam). Then, unpin the waistband. Starting from the edge of the dress that has the excess waistband fabric, slide the waistband fabric through the unpicked seam until it feels comfortable around your waist. When you have a good fit, pin the waistband to the seam. Take off the dress and repin the waistband to the dress along the bottom row of shirring. Then rebaste the waistband seam in place and cut away the excess waistband fabric so it's even with the edge of the dress. If your waistband seems too tight, follow the same steps, but slide the waistband fabric in the opposite direction.

7. Once you're satisfied with the fit of the waistband and the placement of the buttons and buttonholes, resew along the basted seams using a normal stitch length.

8. On the right side of the dress, sew about ¼" from the top of the waistband from one edge of the button/buttonhole plackets to the other, removing pins as you go. Repin the bottom of the waistband to the skirt portion of the dress, pulling skirt gathers straight down, perpendicular to the waistband. Sew along the bottom edge of the waistband in the same manner as you did the top. Backstitch at the beginning and end of both seams. ⑭

9. Starting at the top edge of one side of the dress, sew a tight zigzag stitch along the entire length of the seam to enclose all raw edges. Repeat on the other side of the dress. ⑮

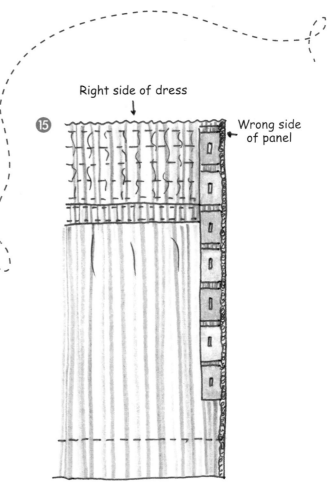

Right side of dress

⑮

Wrong side of panel

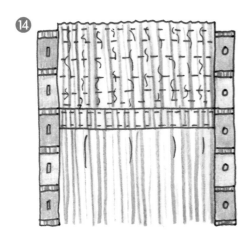

⑭

10. Press the raw edges between the end of the button/ buttonhole plackets and bottom of the dress ¼" toward the wrong side; sew ⅛" from the fold from the end of the plackets to the bottom of the dress.

ADD THE STRAPS

1. Find the center back of the dress and mark it with a safety pin. Try on your dress, adjusting it so the buttonhole placket rests in the middle of your chest. Safety pin the end of your dressmaker's measuring tape to the top of the dress, about 2" from one edge of the placket and ½" down from the top of the dress. Mark this placement with a marking tool on the wrong side of the dress. Rotate the dress around your body 180° so the safety pin on the back rests in the middle of your chest. Pull the measuring tape over your shoulder and pull it taut outside of the back of the dress, about 2½" from the safety pin and ½" down from the top of the dress. Note the measurement on the tape and add ½". This is the measurement you will use for the length of your straps. (My measurement was 12½".) **16**

2. From the remaining sheet fabric, cut a 4½"-wide strip that is twice the length of your strap measurement. With right sides together, sew the two long edges of the strip together to form a tube. Turn the tube inside out; press the seam to the back center of the tube. Sew ¼" from both long edges of the tube. Fold the tube in half widthwise and cut it in half at the fold. These are your straps. **17**

3. Fold and press the short edges of each strap ¼" toward the *right* side of the strap. Using the marked spots on the dress for placement, pin the straps to the dress, aligning the pressed short edge of the strap ½" below the top edge of the dress. Sew a rectangle shape around the edge of the strap to attach it to the dress. Repeat to attach the other strap edges to the dress. **18**

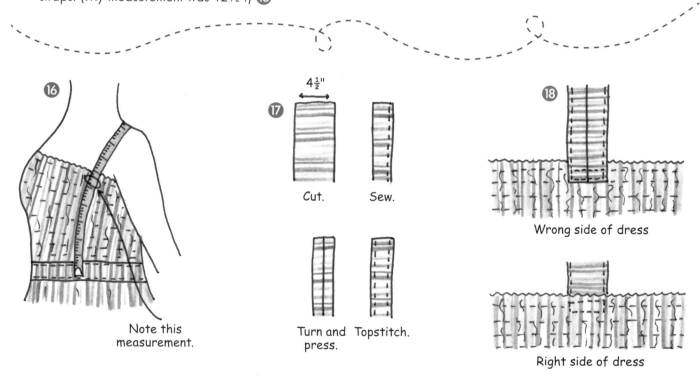

16

Note this measurement.

4½"

17

Cut.   Sew.

Turn and   Topstitch.
press.

18

Wrong side of dress

Right side of dress

Felted and Flapped PURSE

Out thrifting one day, I stumbled across this colorful, 100% wool sweater. The previous owner had shrunken this funky striped pullover to the size of an elementary-schoolgirl's top half. There was no way I could wear it on *my* top half (my elementary-school days are long gone), but I loved the mix of bright pinks and yellows with the muted browns and greens—it struck me as an unusual color palette. So the sweater became mine. After some experimentation, the sweater became a purse!

At first, I wanted this purse to be "the perfectly square purse." But having sewn sweater fabrics before, I knew my purse would never be *perfectly* square. The stretch of sweater fabric simply won't allow it. And that's exactly what I like about this little purse. She flares out at the bottom, where the bottom ribbing of the original sweater falls. She'll gladly stow your plastic, paper, coins, cell phone, and keys. She won't hold moon rocks or liquids. She's just not meant for heavy packing. But a day trip out for some casual fun? She's all about that.

my fiber facts

Size: Women's Large (but shrunk to a Small!)

Content: 100% wool

design diversions

- Use only the body of the sweater in the design; skip the bottom ribbing

- Add beads or buttons to the purse flap, maybe around the button or along the binding

- Instead of a "square" purse shape, sew a triangle that mimics the shape of the flap

- Make the purse wider and shorter

- Make it skinnier and taller

GATHER YOUR MATERIALS

- One men's or women's 100% wool sweater

- Thread to coordinate with sweater fabric

- Large button, or a Cover Button Kit by Dritz (size 60)*

- Fabric-marking tool

- Ruler

- Long pins

- Scissors

- Rotary-cutting equipment (optional but useful)

- Dressmaker's measuring tape

- Hand sewing needle

*Kits to make your own buttons are found at fabric/ sewing stores and typically cost less than $3.00.

CUT AND SEW THE PURSE

1. Felt your sweater following the instructions in "Felting Wool Sweaters" (page 142).

2. Turn the sweater wrong side out and lay it flat, matching up the front and back of the sweater along the bottom edges. Use a marking tool and ruler to draw an 8" x 8" square on the front of the sweater, including the bottom ribbing. From the

center of the top line, measure up 4½" and mark a dot. Draw two diagonal lines to connect the dot with the top two corners of the square. ❶

3. Pin the sweater layers together ½" inside the drawn lines of the "house" shape. Cut on the marked lines through both layers. Unpin the upper triangle portion of the shape, keeping the square part pinned together. Cut away the triangle shape from the top layer only; save it for another use. You should have two pieces: a square and a "house." ❷

4. Pin the two pieces, right sides together. Using a ¼" seam allowance and a straight stitch, sew the three straight sides of the purse. ❸

5. Clip the bottom two corners of the purse close to the stitching and turn it right side out. Roll the seams outward and inward—with your fingers, as if you're using a rolling pin—until all seams lie flat.

CUT AND SEW THE BINDING

1. Measure around the top of the purse. Starting at one side seam, travel up and around the triangle shape and along the top front of the purse to where you began measuring. Your measurement should be approximately 19½". Add 1" to this measurement. ❹

2. Cut one of the sweater sleeves from the remaining sweater piece, following the armhole seams; cut the sleeve open at the sleeve seam and lay it flat. To make the binding strip, cut a 1¼"-wide strip from the sleeve to the measurement from step 1; it should be 1¼" x approximately 20½". Use a zigzag stitch to finish the two long edges of the strip. Do not sew the two short edges. ❺

Note: If your wool is tightly felted, the edges won't ravel and you can skip the zigzag stitching.

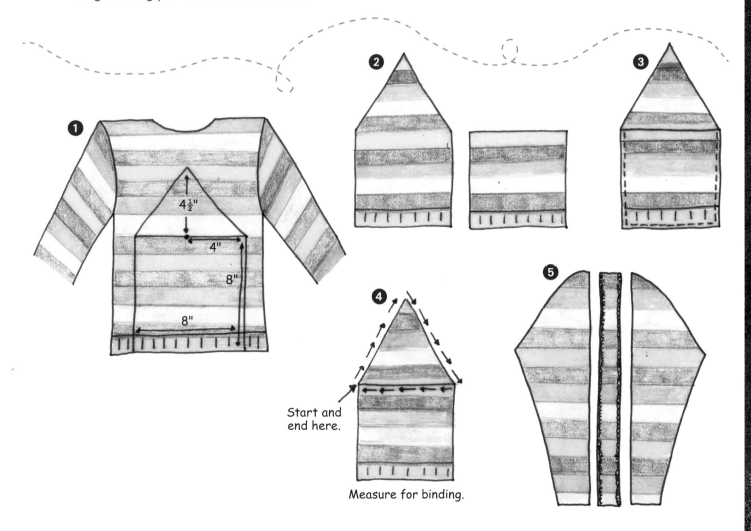

Start and end here.

Measure for binding.

3. With right sides together, begin in the center of the 8"-wide edge of the purse front to pin the binding strip in place. Align the edges and pin the binding across the front of the purse, up one side of the flap, down the other side, and across the remainder of the front of the purse. Overlap the ends of the binding ½" and cut off any excess. ❻

4. Using a ¼" seam allowance and a straight stitch, sew the binding to the purse opening. Start at the beginning of the binding and sew around to the end, backstitching at both ends. ❼

5. Turn the purse wrong side out. Fold the zigzagged edges of the binding toward the wrong side of the purse and turn under ¼"; pin. (If you're confident at sewing, you can turn the zigzag edges under and hold them down as you hand sew rather than pinning.) Hand stitch the binding to the wrong side of the purse opening using doubled thread and a blindstitch. Knot the end of the thread and insert your needle through the looped thread before you take your second stitch to secure the knot. This will keep your knot from popping through the knit. ❽

6. After sewing all the way around the binding, hand stitch the overlapped binding edges together. Knot and cut the thread. To secure the knot, create a large knot in the thread, and then take a tiny stitch; pull the knot through to bury it inside the purse layers. Then take two or three more tiny stitches in place and cut the thread close to the fabric.

RETIP *stitching secret*

When hand sewing, catch just a few threads of the sweater yarn with your needle; don't poke your needle through to the front of the purse. This will ensure that your stitches are hidden.

CUT, SEW, AND ATTACH THE HANDLE

1. To make the handle, cut a 2½" x 15" strip from the sweater sleeve used for the binding. Stitch around all four edges of the rectangle using a zigzag stitch. ❾

2. Fold one long side of the handle strip toward the center by ½" and press. Fold the other side over 1"; turn the zigzag stitches under and press. Sew down the top layer using a straight stitch. For decorative purposes, sew another line of straight stitching about ¼" from the first stitches, so the rows of stitching look centered along the handle. ❿

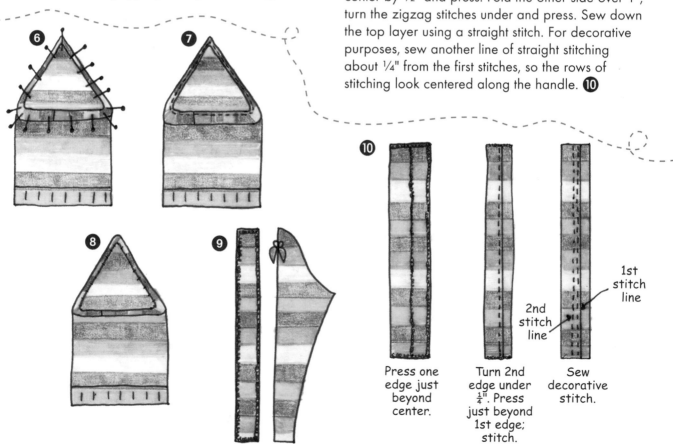

Press one edge just beyond center.

Turn 2nd edge under ¼". Press just beyond 1st edge; stitch.

Sew decorative stitch.

2nd stitch line

1st stitch line

3. Lay the purse on a flat surface, wrong side out. Place the right side of one end of the handle about 1" down from the top of the purse. Position the long edge of the handle against one purse side seam. Turn under the zigzag edge of the handle and pin in place. Using a straight stitch, sew a rectangle shape ⅛" from the edges around the bottom edge of the handle to secure it to the purse. Repeat on the other side of the purse, making sure not to twist the handle. ⑪

SEW THE BUTTONHOLE AND BUTTON

1. If you're making a covered button out of your sweater fabric, do so now, following the kit manufacturer's instructions.

2. Measure the diameter of your button and subtract ¼". With scissors, make a vertical cut to this measurement through the purse flap, referring to the illustration for placement. Sew a zigzag stitch along the two long edges of the cut and a straight stitch along the short edges to secure the edges of the buttonhole and prevent stretching. ⑫

3. Close the flap and position the button in the center of the buttonhole; hand sew the button in place to the front of the purse with doubled thread. Knot and secure your thread.

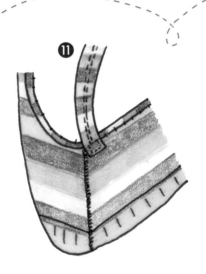

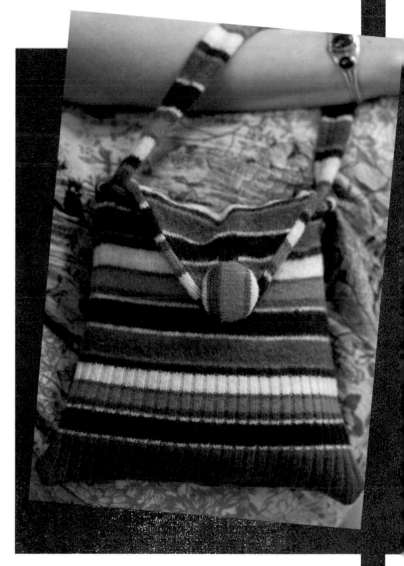

sweater SCARVES

These funky scarves feel as cozy to wear as a sweater! They're also simple to put together—no complex sewing required.

You can change the length, width, and look of your scarf in many ways. Cut your sweater as thriftily as possible to keep your options open. For a longer or shorter scarf, increase or decrease the number of squares you sew together (keep the final total an even number). For the women's scarf, I used the blue ribbing around the bottom of the sweater as a design accent. I cut four squares from the ribbing and used them on each end of the scarf. If there are unique details you would like to transfer from your sweater to your scarf, cut the required number of squares from those areas.

Women's scarf about 80" long; men's scarf about 68" long.

my fiber facts

Size: Women's Medium (for women's scarf);
Men's XL (for men's scarf)

Content: 100% wool

design diversions

- Measure the length and width of your favorite scarf and replicate those measurements in your sweater scarf
- Appliqué smaller squares to each pair of squares along the scarf for added dimension
- Add beads, buttons, or embroidery to the women's scarf
- Add simple, dark embroidered details to the men's scarf

GATHER YOUR MATERIALS

- One men's or women's sweater, at least 70% wool
- Thread to match sweater fabric
- Scissors
- Rotary-cutting equipment (optional but useful)
- Ruler
- Long pins
- Blunt tool (for turning)
- Thin cloth (for damp pressing)
- Hand sewing needle

CUT THE SWEATER

1. Lay the sweater flat, right side out. Use scissors to cut the sweater along the side seams, armhole seams, and shoulder seams. The back and front should now be two separate pieces; the sleeves should be separated from the body of the sweater. **1**

2. Straighten one edge of the sweater front and back by cutting with scissors or rotary-cutting equipment, using the stripes or stitches in the knitted fabric as a guide. Cut squares referring to the chart below. Use fabric from the sweater sleeves, if needed, to obtain the desired number of squares. **2**

SCARF	NUMBER OF SQUARES TO CUT	SIZE OF SQUARES
Women's	50	3½" x 3½"
Men's	32	4½" x 4½"

SEW THE SCARF

1. Lay half of the squares side by side to create the front of the scarf (25 squares for women, 16 squares for men); alternate the direction of the knitted fabric from square to square.

2. With right sides together, pin and sew the first two squares together along one side using a ¼" seam allowance and a straight stitch. Sew the next two squares together in the same manner. Continue sewing the squares into pairs; when completed, pin and sew the pairs into one long strip. **3**

3. Repeat steps 1 and 2 to create the back of the scarf.

Note: You'll likely find that your sweater fabric stretches a bit, even if you use a stretch stitch on your machine. That's okay here! The bit of stretch that the sewing creates makes for a slightly skewed look, which is the goal. If you find that your sweater fabric stretches into points with each sewn seam, simply trim those points so they're even with the square fabric again. **4**

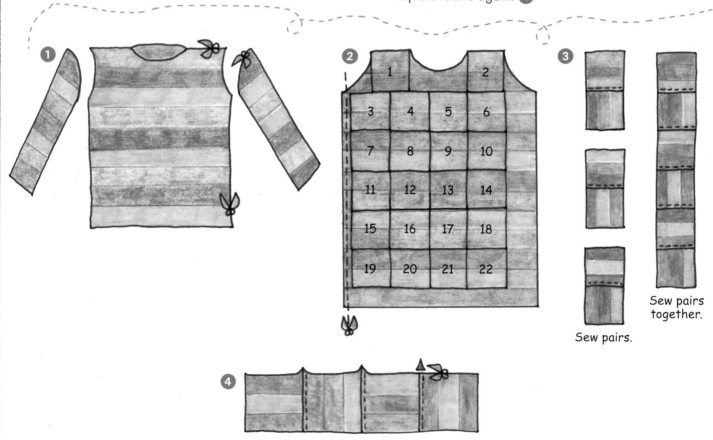

Sew pairs.

Sew pairs together.

Trim points even.

4. Lay the front and back of the scarf, right sides together, on a flat surface. Match the seams and pin through the scarf layers on either side of each seam, so the seam allowances are pinned open. Starting about 1" from the corner on a short side, sew around the scarf using a straight stitch and a ¼" seam allowance. Backstitch at each end; leave a 2" opening on one short side for turning. **5**

5. Turn the scarf right side out. Use a blunt tool (such as the bottom of a pen or pencil) to push the corners into points. Lay the scarf on a flat surface and roll the seams outward and inward—with your fingers, as if you're using a rolling pin—until all seams lie flat. Place a damp cloth over the scarf (a thin cotton dish towel or scrap of fabric is fine) and press with an iron to temporarily fix the squares in place and flatten the fabric for sewing. Turn the edges of the 2" opening ¼" to the inside and pin. Hand sew the 2" opening closed using a whipstitch (page 140).

6. Pin through the layers of each short seam along the length of the scarf to stabilize the squares for sewing. Using a straight stitch and a longer-than-normal stitch length, sew a square shape ½" inside each square, backstitching at each end. **6**

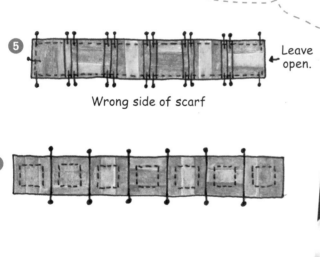

5 Leave open.

Wrong side of scarf

6

five-square PURSE

The sweater I used here is only 80% wool, which means that parts will fray when cut (in this case, certain rows of the knitted fabric fray and certain rows don't). Choosing a sweater that is less than 100% wool is fine, but expect some fraying and stretching. Hold fraying rows with dots of Fray Check, which is commonly found at fabric stores and lasts through multiple washings. To prevent extra stretching, read "Sewing Sweaters" (page 141), where I've listed several tips to try.

my fiber facts

Size: Women's Large

Content: 80% wool, 20% acrylic

design diversions

- Add an entirely different appliquéd motif to the front of the purse
- Add appliquéd motifs to the back of the purse as well
- Round the bottom edges of the purse
- Round the corners of the handles
- Add beads, buttons, or yarn embroidery

GATHER YOUR MATERIALS

- One 100% wool or wool-blend sweater
- Thread to match sweater fabric
- Ruler or dressmaker's measuring tape
- Fabric-marking tool
- Long pins
- Scissors
- Rotary-cutting equipment (optional but useful)
- Fray Check (optional)
- Hand-sewing needle

CUT AND SEW THE PURSE

1. Felt the sweater, following the instructions in "Felting Wool Sweaters" (page 142).

2. Turn the felted sweater inside out and lay it on a flat surface with the bottom edges aligned. Measure and mark a 10" x 10¼" rectangle on the front of the sweater, aligning the bottom edge of the rectangle you draw with the bottom of the sweater. Pin through both layers of the sweater, ½" inside the drawn lines. ❶

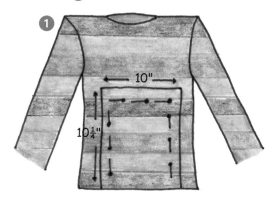

FIVE-SQUARE PURSE

PURSE PART	NUMBER OF SQUARES TO CUT	SIZE OF SQUARES
Handles	4	5½" x 5½"
Large appliqué	1	4½" x 4½"
Small appliqué	2	2" x 2"

3. Using scissors or rotary-cutting equipment, cut out the rectangle just inside the drawn lines through both layers.

4. Using a ¼" seam allowance and a short straight stitch, sew around the sides and bottom of the rectangle. Backstitch at the beginning and end. Leave the top of the rectangle open. Remove pins. ❷

   Note: You may want to use a zigzag stitch if your sweater isn't 100% wool to prevent fraying on the inside of the purse.

5. Turn the purse right side out and lay it on a flat surface. Roll the seams outward and inward—with your fingers, as if you're using a rolling pin—until all seams lie flat.

CUT AND SEW HANDLES AND APPLIQUÉS

1. From the remaining sweater fabric, cut squares referring to the chart at right. Start with the fabric left over from the front and back of the sweater, and then use the sleeves if needed.

2. Mark a 2" square in the center of the handle pieces (1¾" from the sides). Fold the square in half and cut a slit inside the markings with scissors. Insert your scissors into the slit and carefully cut the square shape out of the center, just outside the drawn lines.

3. Repeat step 2 to cut out a 1" square from the center of the large square appliqué (1¾" from the sides) and a ½" square from the two small square appliqués (¾" from the sides). ❸

4. Lay two handle pieces on top of one another, *wrong* sides together, and pin. Using a tight straight stitch and a ¼" seam allowance, sew around the outside of the handles. Then, sew using a ¼" seam allowance around the cutout square on the inside of the handles. Repeat with the other two handle pieces. Use Fray Check along the edges of the handle if your wool isn't tightly felted or if the fiber content isn't 100% wool. ❹

Handles

Large square

Small squares

5. Center one handle from side to side along the top front of the purse. Align the top of the purse with the bottom edge of the cutout square; pin in place. Using a tight straight stitch, sew the handle to the front of purse, following the previously sewn seams on the handle. Attach the second handle to the back of the purse in the same manner. **5**

6. Hand sew the outer layers of the handles together using a whipstitch (page 140); when you reach the layers on top of the purse, add the purse layer to your stitches. Whipstitch the layers of the cutout squares together. Refer to "Sewing Sweaters: Hand Sewing" (page 142) for tips. **6**

7. Center the large square appliqué on the front of the purse; pin. Hand appliqué the outer edges of the square to the front of the purse using a blind stitch (page 140). Appliqué the cutout square edges to the front of the purse.

8. Pin the small square appliqués to the front of the purse as shown or where desired. Appliqué the outside edges of the squares to the front of the purse, and then the cutout square edges. **7**

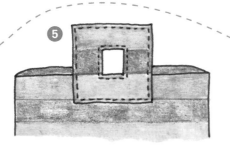

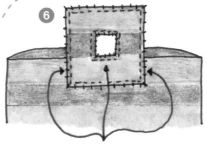

Whipstitch through
all three layers here.

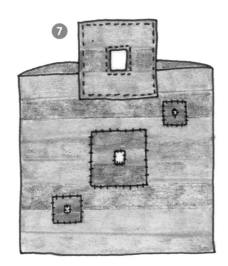

eco Tote

Just about everybody I know has a collection of reusable totes for their weekly grocery-store visits. But what about a smaller, sturdier tote for all of the other places you frequent? Farmer's market, bookstore, fabric store, thrift shop, library—we cart items out of these places all the time, often in a one-time-use bag. Strong, durable corduroy is the perfect fabric for an all-purpose tote that will get a lot of use. Drop your wallet, phone, and keys into this stylish tote, and you can pick up whatever you need while leaving the one-use bag behind.

my fiber facts

Size: Men's 34" x 33"; Men's 38" x 32"

Content: 100% cotton; 84% polyester, 16% nylon

design diversions

- Embroider an earth-friendly image (like a tree or flower) in place of the buttons

- Use two completely different colors, instead of two values of the same color

- Make longer handles so the tote top hits at your waist, for some extra swing

- Add a simple pocket to the back or inside of the purse to hold a wallet or cell phone

- Sew your initials in buttons

GATHER YOUR MATERIALS

- Two pairs of men's corduroy pants* in dark and light values of the same color

- Assorted small- to medium-sized buttons that coordinate with pants fabrics

- Thread to coordinate with pants fabrics

- Seam ripper

- Scissors

- Rotary-cutting equipment (optional but useful)

- Ruler or dressmaker's measuring tape

- Long pins

- Cardstock or lightweight cardboard (for templates)

- Fabric-marking tool

- Hand-sewing needle

- Long, blunt tool (for turning)

*Pant legs must be at least 32½" long and 8½" wide to follow this tote design to the letter. Of course, there are ways to adjust the pattern slightly to fit your thrift-store finds. You can cut the center panel narrower or shorten the length of all three panels so your specific corduroys will work. If you cut carefully, you may be able to get a second tote from your two pairs of pants.

CUT THE PANTS

1. Turn the light-colored pants inside out; use a seam ripper to unpick cuff hems if needed. Unpick the pant-leg seams on both sides of one pant leg, up to the waistband and up to the top of the inseam; cut the front and back apart, following the front opening and waistband seams. Cut away and discard the pocket linings.

ECO TOTE

2. With scissors or rotary-cutting equipment, straighten one long side of the front pant leg by following the "stripes" (or wale) in the corduroy fabric; begin cutting at the narrow bottom end. Measure and cut two 5" x 13¾" rectangles from the front fabric; measure and cut one 8½" x 32½" rectangle from the back fabric. **1**

RETIP *rip as desired*

As you might have discovered, corduroy is *not* a delicate fabric. If you need to unpick a seam, start by unpicking a few stitches, and then take one end of the fabric in each hand and try to rip the seam apart. The seam may or may not rip easily, but it won't hurt the fabric to try—and if you succeed at ripping, it will save a lot of cutting and/or unpicking time.

3. Repeat step 1 to prepare the dark-colored pants for cutting. Cut two 5" x 32½" rectangles, one from the front fabric and one from the back fabric. **2**

SEW THE TOTE

1. With right sides together, pin and sew one long side of one dark-colored rectangle to one long side of the light-colored rectangle using a straight stitch and a ¼" seam allowance. Sew the other dark-colored rectangle to the opposite side of the light-colored rectangle in the same manner. **3**

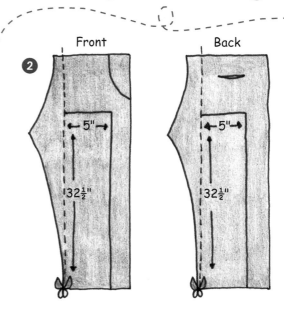

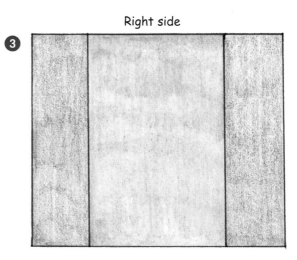

Straightening cuts

2. Fold one dark-colored rectangle toward the light-colored rectangle, *wrong* sides together, along the seam. Roll the seam outward and inward—with your fingers, as if you're using a rolling pin—until the seam lies flat; pin. Sew using a ¼" seam allowance along the pinned edge. Repeat for the other seam. Finger-press the seams toward the light corduroy. This creates a decorative seam on the outside of the tote and encloses the raw edges of the seams on the inside. ➍

3. Fold the long side of each dark brown rectangle to find the center and mark with a pin. Fold and mark the center of one 5" side of *each* 5" x 13¾" light-colored rectangle. With right sides together, match up the two center marks and pin. With right sides together—so your tote looks like it is inside out—pin the long edges of the tote side (light-colored rectangle) to the edges of the tote body (two-toned piece). Leave the tote bottom unpinned except for the center marking pin. Repeat on the other side. ➎

4. Using a straight stitch and a ¼" seam allowance, sew the pinned long edges of one tote side to the tote body. Remove pins as you sew. Backstitch at the beginning and end of each seam. Repeat on the other side of the tote.

5. Remove the tote from your machine. On one tote side with right sides together, fold the long edges you just sewed toward the center of the bag, align the edges of the tote bottom, and pin. Cut a small diagonal slit where the corners of the fabric meet to flatten the seam for sewing. Make sure not to cut into the sewn seams. Sew using a ¼" seam allowance along the bottom edge, taking care that you don't sew in any puckers or folds. Backstitch at each end. ➏

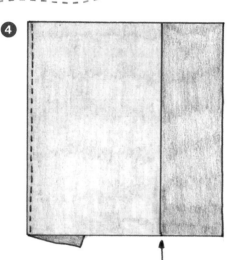

Repeat with this seam.

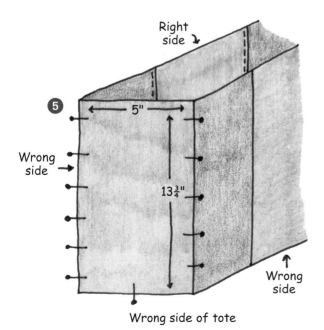

Right side ↘

➎

5"

13¾"

Wrong side →

Wrong side

Wrong side of tote

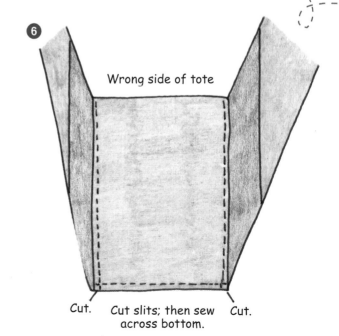

➏

Wrong side of tote

Cut. Cut slits; then sew Cut.
across bottom.

6. Turn the tote right side out. With *wrong* sides together, fold one side edge of the tote front together; roll the seam outward and inward—with your fingers, as if you're using a rolling pin—until the seam lies flat. Pin the seam through both layers of the tote along the edge in preparation for sewing. Repeat the folding and rolling along the bottom of the tote front and up the other side of the tote front. When all three sides are rolled flat and pinned, sew using a ¼" seam allowance along all three sides, pivoting the tote 90° at each corner. Be sure that the intersecting vertical seams are facing the center of the tote. As in step 2, this creates a decorative seam on the outside of the tote and encloses the raw edges of the seam allowances on the inside. **7**

7. Repeat step 6 to sew a seam around the sides and bottom of the tote back.

8. Roll and pin the two bottom side seams of the tote and sew ¼" from the edge from beginning to end. **8**

9. Turn the tote inside out. Fold and press the top edge ½" toward the inside of the bag all around. Fold the top edge toward the inside of the bag another 1"; press and pin. Sew ¼" from the edge of the pressed fold *and* sew ¼" from the top folded edge. **9**

EMBELLISH THE TOTE

1. From the remaining dark corduroy fabric, cut a 4½" x 8½" rectangle, with the "stripes" of the corduroy following the *length* of the rectangle. Center the dark rectangle on the light panel on the front of the tote; pin. Stitch ¼" from the edges all around the rectangle, leaving the raw edges of the fabric exposed.

2. From the remaining light corduroy fabric, cut a 3½" x 7½" rectangle, with the "stripes" in the corduroy following the *width* of the rectangle.

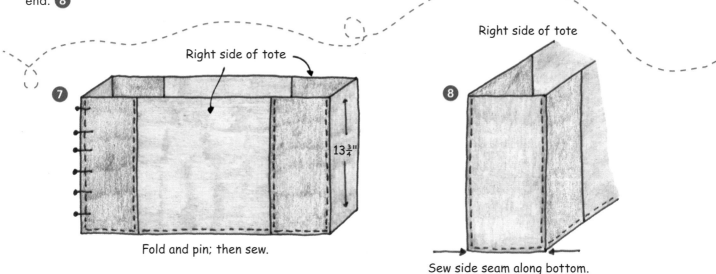

7 Right side of tote

13¾"

Fold and pin; then sew.

8 Right side of tote

Sew side seam along bottom.

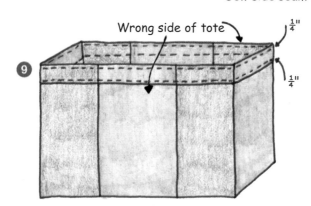

9 Wrong side of tote

¼"

¼"

3. Make templates from lightweight cardboard or cardstock using the "r" and "e" letter patterns (on the facing page). Use the templates and a fabric-marking tool to trace the letters onto the light corduroy rectangle. (Or draw letters freehand on the fabric in your own style.)

4. Hand sew assorted buttons to fill in the traced lines, making sure the buttons are at least ½" from the edges of the rectangle.

5. Center the light rectangle on top of the dark rectangle and pin. Stitch around the light rectangle, ¼" from the edges, leaving the raw edges of the fabric exposed.

CUT AND SEW HANDLES

1. From the remaining light corduroy fabric, cut twelve 2½" x 4½" rectangles, with the "stripes" of the corduroy following the *width* of the rectangles. Cut eight 2½" x 4½" rectangles from the remaining dark corduroy fabric, also with the stripes following the *width* of the rectangles.

2. Arrange the cut rectangles in four rows of five rectangles each, alternating light and dark fabrics. Sew the short edges of the rectangles together using a ¼" seam allowance to make four long strips. Finger-press the seam allowances in one direction. ⑩

3. With right sides together, lay one strip on top of another, rotating the strips as needed so that the pressed seam allowances lie in opposite directions and bump together. Pin the strips together on either side of each seam. Using a straight stitch and a ¼" seam allowance, sew around the strip, leaving a 1½" opening on one short end for turning. Backstitch at the beginning and end. Trim the fabric diagonally at the four corners, close to the stitching, to reduce bulk. Repeat to make the second handle. ⑪

4. Turn the handles right side out. It helps to use a long, blunt tool (such as the handle end of a wooden spoon) to push the fabric through the hole. Roll the seams outward and inward—with your fingers, as if you're using a rolling pin—until the seams lie flat. (I found ironing to be almost useless on the sewn seams of my corduroy fabric. But give it a try to see if you prefer it to the rolling method.) Fold the raw edges ¼" toward the inside of the handle and pin. Hand sew the opening closed using a whipstitch (page 140).

⑩

Make 4.

⑪

Trim corners.

Leave open.

RETIP *grab your toolbox*

You may have an especially handy tool for turning your handles inside out right at your fingertips—pliers. As long as the pliers are clean, blunt-tipped, and blunt-bladed (meaning they don't cut, only grip), you can use them to pull the fabric out of the opening instead of pushing it through. I *don't* recommend using pliers with more delicate fabrics, but for me, pliers made the time-consuming task of turning these corduroy tubes right side out a cinch.

5. Pin the fabric layers on one handle together so they lie flat. Using a straight stitch, sew ¼" from the edges all around the handle. Repeat for the other handle. 🅬

6. Place the end of one handle inside the tote front, aligning it with the bottom of the hem and the vertical seam of a dark corduroy panel. Pin and sew using a short, straight stitch. Sew over the stitching on the handle to within ¼" of the top edge of the tote; then sew across the width of the handle in a rectangle shape. Repeat to attach the other end of the handle to the opposite side of the tote, making sure not to twist the handle. Attach the other handle to the tote in the same manner. 🅭 🅮

🅬

🅭

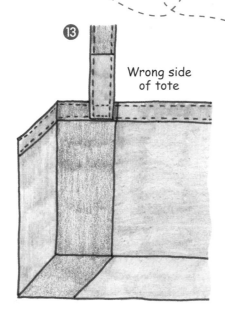

Wrong side of tote

🅮

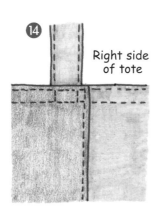

Right side of tote

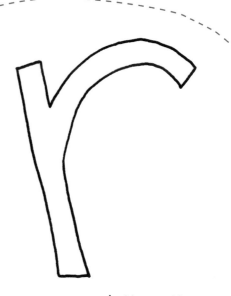

Letter patterns

newsboy Cap and Scarf set

I bought this sweater long ago at a thrift store. I loved it and thought it was beautiful. After several months of taking it out, trying it on, and putting it back on the closet shelf, I finally admitted that it just didn't fit me right. But I couldn't donate it back to the thrift store. Oh no! I designed a cap and scarf set with this particular sweater in mind. The stripes get put to good use in both pieces.

One size fits most for the cap. As long as one sleeve is long enough to wrap comfortably around your neck, you can tailor the scarf size as desired. One tip before you start: It's important that your thread match your sweater fabric in this project. If yours is a multicolored sweater, try to find a variegated thread that coordinates.

my fiber facts

Size: Women's Large

Content: 50% acrylic, 44% mohair, 6% wool

design diversions

- Use the second sleeve to make the scarf longer
- Use sweater leftovers to make a pair of child's mittens (page 116)
- Trace your own hands to make a pair of adult-sized mittens

GATHER YOUR MATERIALS

- One women's large-size long-sleeved sweater
- Thread to match sweater
- Approximately 1 yard of acrylic yarn (any color, as the yarn will be hidden)
- Large button, or a Cover Button Kit by Dritz (size 60)*
- Scissors
- Template material (such as a cereal box, a shoebox, or heavy cardstock)
- Fabric-marking tool
- Long pins
- Dressmaker's measuring tape
- Template plastic (found at quilt shops, fabric stores, and craft stores)
- Hand sewing needle
- Safety pin

*Kits to make your own buttons are found at fabric/ sewing stores and usually cost less than $3.00.

MAKE THE CAP AND BAND

1. Use scissors to cut along the side seams and armhole fronts of the sweater; then cut along the shoulder seams and across the neckline to cut the sweater front away from the rest of the garment.

2. Use the cap pattern (page 111) to make a template from cardboard or cardstock. Use the template and a fabric-marking tool to trace the shape onto the front of the sweater seven times. Refer to "ReTip: Matching Patterns" (below) if sweater is striped. Cut out the seven cap pieces on the drawn lines. **1**

3. Sew a zigzag stitch along the two long edges of each cap piece to prevent unraveling.

RETIP *matching patterns*

If there are patterns or textures in your sweater you'd like to show off on your cap, cut the cap pieces to match each other. You can use one sleeve of the sweater if needed. If you want to use the back of the sweater, cut out the cap brim first; see "Make and Attach the Brim," step 1 (page 108).

4. Place two cap pieces right sides together, edges matching; pin one long side. Sew the pinned sides together using a straight stitch or a straight stretch stitch and a ¼" seam allowance. Backstitch at the beginning and end of the seam. Sew all seven pieces together to make a strip; then pin and sew the first piece to the last piece to form the cap top. (There will be a small hole in the top of your cap, but don't worry we'll close that up later.) **2**

5. Sew a zigzag stitch around the bottom of the cap to prevent unraveling.

6. Fold one of the cap seams so the pieces on each side of the seam meet, *wrong* sides together. Pin together along the bottom of the seam; measure up 1½" and insert another pin. Sew from the bottom of the seam to the 1½" mark using a straight stitch and a ¼" seam allowance, essentially encasing the zigzag seam inside. Backstitch at the beginning and end of the stitching. Repeat on the other six seams. These "tucks" will create a gathered look above the cap band. **3**

7. Measure your head circumference (mine was 22"); add ½" to your measurement. From one of the sleeves of the sweater, cut a strip that measures 2½" x your final head-circumference measurement. (My strip measured 2½" x 22½".) Wrap the strip around your head, positioning it where you want the band of your cap to sit. Overlap the short ends by ¼". If the band seems a little loose, you can cut a bit off of one short side of the strip and try it on again. Once you get a good fit (snug, but not tight), sew a zigzag stitch along both *long* edges of the strip. With right sides together and a zigzag stitch, sew the short ends of the strip together to form a ring. **4**

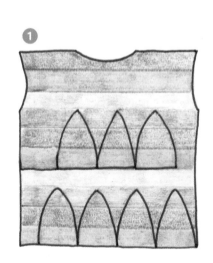

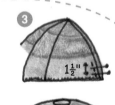

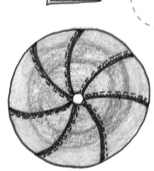

8. Choose one of the seven cap pieces for the front of the cap and insert a pin on the raw edge of this piece to mark the center front. Hold the pin in one hand and fold the fabric around it; pull the cap taut so the two layers lie flat. Insert a pin into the opposite edge to mark the center back. Now, match up the two pins by folding the cap again; mark the opposite two edges with pins for the sides. Your cap should be divided into four equal parts. **5**

9. Repeat the folding process to divide the cap band from step 7 into four equal parts, using the seam as one placeholder. **6**

10. Place the cap top and cap band right sides together, so that the band seam is at the center back of the cap. Match the remaining three sets of pins and pin the layers together. Add pins between the four pins, easing the cap fabric as needed. **7**

11. Starting at the band seam, sew just inside the zigzag stitches around the cap top to secure the cap band to the cap top. With the cap wrong side out, turn the zigzagged edge of the cap band ¼" toward the inside of the cap *two times*, pinning as

you go around, to encase the zigzagged edge inside the fabric. Using a blind stitch (page 140), hand sew the turned edge closed. **8**

MAKE AND ATTACH THE BRIM

1. Trace the brim pattern (page 111) onto template plastic and cut it out. Fold the back of the sweater widthwise, right sides together. Trace the brim template onto the folded sweater, a generous ½" from the fold. Pay attention to the stripe placement if your sweater is striped as mine was. **9**

2. Sew a straight stitch or a straight stretch stitch just *outside* of the drawn curved line, beginning and ending just beyond the points of the curve. Leave the inner curved edge unsewn.

3. Cut ¼" beyond your stitches along the *outside* curve of the brim. Then cut ½" from the *inside* curve, following the brim shape from corner to corner. Sew a zigzag stitch along both sides of the *inside* curve to prevent unraveling (do not sew these edges together; sew them each separately). **10**

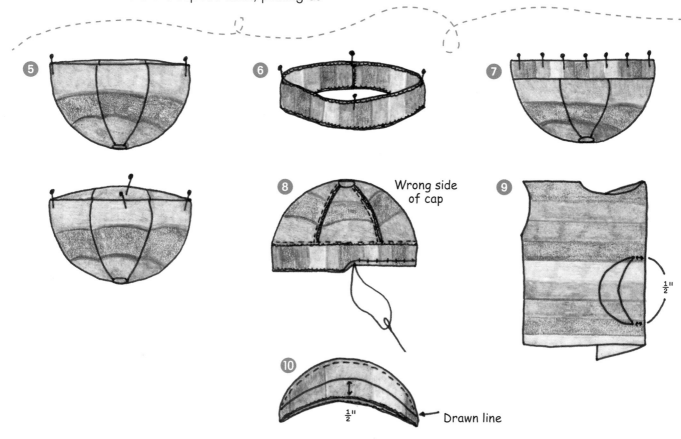

Wrong side of cap

½"

½"

Drawn line

4. Turn the brim right side out and roll the seams so they lie flat. Insert the plastic brim template inside the fabric brim. Pull the fabric taut against the outer edge of the plastic brim and pin in place just beyond the inner curve of the brim template. ⑪

5. Using a straight stitch or a straight stretch stitch, sew the two layers of the *inside* curve together as close to the plastic brim as you can, enclosing the plastic brim inside the fabric brim. ⑫

6. Find the center front of the cap (opposite the band seam) and the center front of the brim; insert a pin at these two points as placeholders. Place the brim and the center front of the cap right sides together along the edges and match up the pins. Pin the band and the brim together. Using a straight stitch or a straight stretch stitch and a ¼" seam allowance, sew the brim to the cap band. Use lots of pins and sew slowly for best results. ⑬

CLOSE UP THE TOP

1. Cut away any pointed ends at the opening on the top of the cap to make a nice, even circle. Sew a zigzag stitch around the opening to prevent unraveling. Turn the cap inside out. Turn the top edge of the opening about ½" toward the inside of the cap and pin. Hand sew the turned edge down using a blind stitch (page 140), leaving a ½" opening, to create a casing for gathering the cap at the top. Keep the thread and needle in position on the cap; do not knot or cut the thread yet. ⑭

2. Tie the ends of the acrylic yarn together to create a knot. Thread a safety pin through the knot. Feed the safety pin through the ½" opening and into the casing. Pull the yarn though the casing by gathering fabric onto the safety pin and then slipping the gathered fabric past the pin. Keep gathering until the safety pin reaches the ½" opening. Pull the safety pin out of the casing; then pull both ends of the yarn tight to close the opening. Knot the two ends of yarn together to form one big knot, trim the excess yarn, and slip the knot inside the casing. Hand sew the ½" opening of the casing closed with the needle and thread.

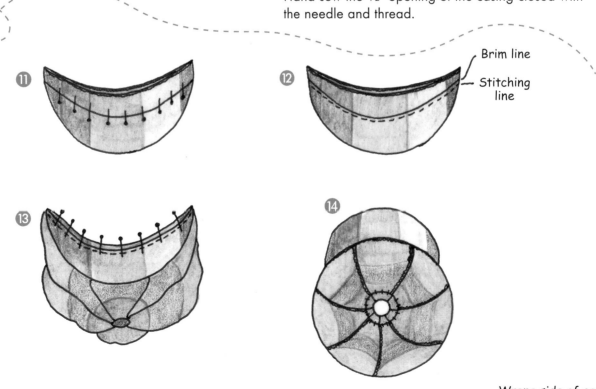

Brim line

Stitching line

Wrong side of cap

NEWSBOY SCARF

1. Cut one sleeve of the sweater away from the body of the sweater, turn inside out, and lay flat, keeping the sleeve seam to one side. Draw a 4"-wide rectangle that runs the length of the sleeve. Pin ½" inside the rectangle, pinning all the way around the shape and making sure to pin through both layers of the sleeve. Cut out the rectangle along the drawn lines. ⑮

2. Determine the length of your scarf by wrapping the sleeve rectangle around your neck. Note where the button should fall and estimate how much scarf length you would like to show below the button. Mark this point, and measure; then add 1" for seam allowances. Trim the rectangle to this length. You can include the ribbing if your sweater has it or cut it away as desired. (My rectangle was about 18" long with seam allowances.)

3. Starting 1" from a corner on one short end, sew a straight stitch or a straight stretch stitch around the rectangle using a ¼" seam allowance. Stop when you are about 2" from the beginning stitches. Backstitch at the beginning and end. ⑯

4. Turn the scarf inside out through the 2" opening; then place the scarf on a flat surface and roll the seams inward and outward until they lie flat. Turn the edges of the opening toward the inside of the scarf by ¼" and hand sew the opening closed using a blind stitch (page 140). Using a straight stitch, sew ¼" from the edge all around the scarf. ⑰

5. Wrap the scarf around your neck, overlapping the edges until comfortably snug. Use a safety pin to mark the placement of the button.

6. If you're making a covered button out of your sweater fabric, do so now, following the kit manufacturer's instructions.

7. Measure the diameter of your button and subtract ¼". With scissors, make a cut to this measurement centered across the width of the scarf, where you want the buttonhole placement. Be sure to cut through both layers of the scarf. Sew a zigzag stitch along the two long edges of the cut and a straight stitch along the two short edges to secure the edges of the buttonhole and prevent stretching. ⑱

8. Try on the scarf. Mark the placement of the button on the opposite edge of the scarf with a safety pin. Hand sew the button in place with doubled thread. See "Sewing Sweaters: Hand Sewing" (page 142) for help, if needed.

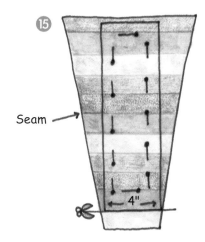

⑮

Seam

4"

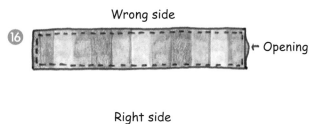

Wrong side

⑯

← Opening

Right side

⑰

⑱

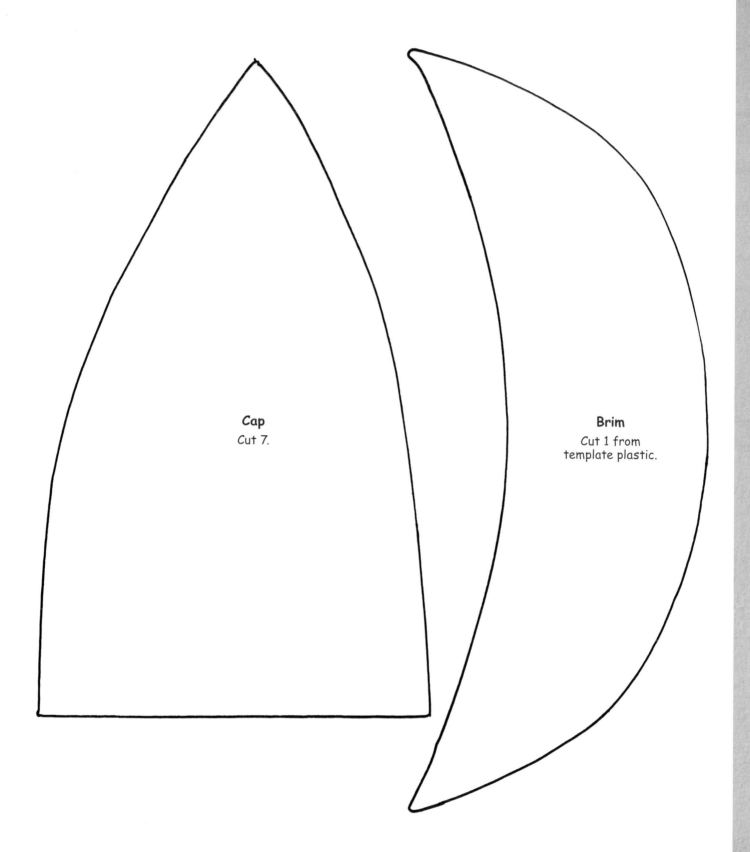

Cap
Cut 7.

Brim
Cut 1 from
template plastic.

happy HAT, MITTEN, and SCARF set

The bright happy colors and stripes in this women's sweater reminded me of my six-year-old son, Jack, so I turned it into Jack's happy hat, mittens, and scarf!

To make all three projects, thrift the biggest sweater you can find. Choose a stretchy sweater that looks similar on the inside and outside (such as one that is entirely ribbed). For just one or two of the projects, a smaller sweater might do fine; read through the instructions before you shop to get an idea of how much sweater fabric you'll need per project. I'm now on the lookout for a sweater that will suit little Charlie, my two-year old. What colors do you think a brazen daredevil might wear?

my fiber facts

Size: Women's XL

Content: 100% cotton

design diversions

- Use a solid-colored sweater and embroider initials, snowflakes, or other details with decorative yarn
- Trace your own hands to make a pair of adult-sized mittens
- Use different, but coordinating, colors of sweaters for the set; unify them with the yarn

GATHER YOUR MATERIALS

- One women's extra-large sweater in a child's favorite colors*
- Thread to match sweater
- Yarn to match or coordinate with sweater (for decorative stitching)
- 30" length of acrylic or other sturdy yarn (any color, as the yarn will be hidden)
- Scissors
- Dressmaker's measuring tape or length of yarn
- Long pins
- Hand sewing needle
- Large-eye needle**
- Large safety pin
- Fabric-marking tool
- Freezer paper
- Long, blunt tool (for turning)

*Most any close-knit fiber will do, although I would shy away from 100% wool if the project is for a child. Wool can become itchy and isn't machine washable.

**The eye of the needle should be large enough for the yarn.

HAPPY HAT

1. Cut along the side seams of your sweater and cut away the sleeves. Cut the front from the back along the shoulder seams. **1**

2. Use a dressmaker's measuring tape or a length of yarn to measure around the widest part of the child's head, starting at the forehead; add 1" to this measurement for the circumference. Measure from the child's eyebrows to the top of his or her head; add 1" to this measurement for the length. Cut a rectangle from the front of your sweater using your two measurements. **2**

   Note: Do not cut off the finished edge at the bottom of the sweater; it will become the bottom of your hat.

3. Using a zigzag stitch, sew along the top long edge of the rectangle to prevent unraveling. You may find that your rectangle stretches—particularly if you're using a ribbed sweater—but that's okay here.

4. Fold the rectangle in half widthwise, right sides together, so both short edges meet. Pin and sew along this seam using a zigzag stitch to create a tube. If you're working with a striped sweater, pin so the stripes match along the seam. **3**

5. Turn down the top edge of the tube ½" toward the wrong side of the sweater fabric. Press. Using a straight stitch and matching thread, sew the turned edge, just inside the zigzag stitching. Leave a 1" opening and backstitch at each end. This creates a casing for gathering the hat at the top. **4**

6. Knot the ends of the 30" length of yarn so that it's doubled, and insert a large safety pin through the knot. Feed the safety pin through the 1" opening of the casing. Pull the yarn though the casing by gathering fabric onto the safety pin, and then slipping the gathered fabric past the pin. Continue gathering until the safety pin emerges from the other side of the 1" opening. Pull both ends of the yarn tight; knot the yarn together and slip the knot inside the casing. Hand sew the 1" opening closed using a whipstitch (page 140).

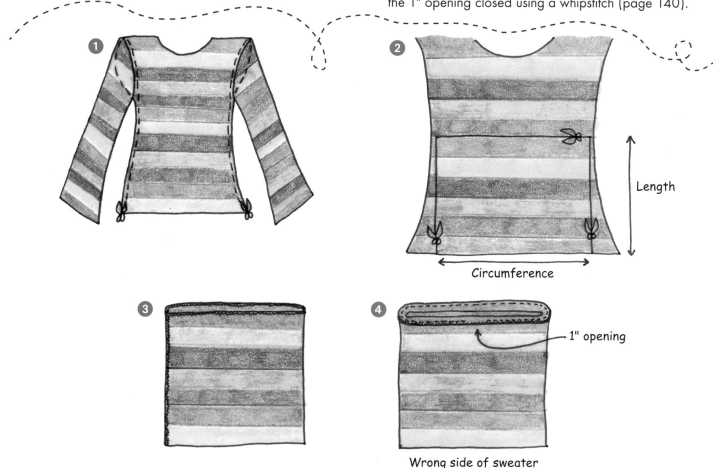

Length

Circumference

1" opening

Wrong side of sweater

Your hat may have a small- or medium-sized hole at the top after you have knotted your yarn tight; it all depends on the size of the hat you're making, the thickness of the knit, and the fiber content. If the hole is closed tight, great! You can go straight to step 7. If not, follow these two additional steps.

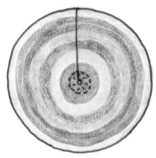

View from cap top, right side out

No hole

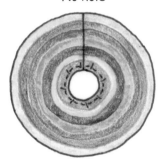

Hole

1. Measure the diameter of the hole at the top of your hat; add 1" to this measurement. Draw and cut out a circle from the original sweater scraps to approximately this diameter. (Go to your kitchen and measure the diameter of your cans, cups, or spice lids—you'll likely find a circle close to the size you need for tracing.) Sew a zigzag stitch around the circle to prevent unraveling.

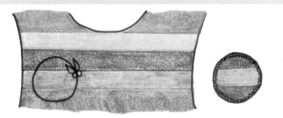

2. Turn the hat inside out. Center the circle wrong side up over the hole. Using a hand sewing needle and doubled thread, hand sew the edge of the circle to the hat using a whipstitch (page 140). Catch just a few threads of the sweater yarn with your needle to hide your stitches; don't poke your needle through to the right side of the hat. Turn the hat right side out and whipstitch the edges of the circle to the gathered fabric. See "Sewing Sweaters: Hand Sewing" (page 142) for help, if needed.

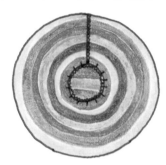

Whipstitch circle to wrong side.

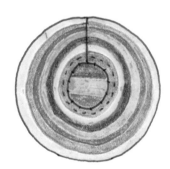

Whipstitch circle to gathered edge on right side.

7. Turn up the brim 1" toward the *right* side of the hat; press. Pin the pressed edge to the right side of the hat and hand sew using a whipstitch (page 140). ⑤

8. Thread the matching or coordinating yarn onto the large-eye needle. You can use a doubled length or single length of yarn, depending on your yarn and the finished look you want. (I used a single strand.) Knot the yarn and starting at the back seam of the hat, poke the needle between the brim and hat layers. Come up through the brim fabric about ¼" from the top of the brim; pull the knot so it is buried between the layers. Insert the needle directly below your first stitch, about ¼" from the bottom of the hat, going through the brim fabric only. Bring the needle out through the brim fabric about ¼" to the left of the top of your first stitch (¼" to the right for left-handers). Repeat until you have embroidered the entire brim. Knot the yarn and bury the knot between the layers. ⑥

HAPPY MITTENS

1. Trace one of the child's hands onto the dull side of freezer paper, starting at the wrist, 1" beyond where you want the mitten to begin. Add ¼" all around as you draw. Keep the child's fingers together and the thumb flared at a 45° angle. Make one more freezer-paper template of the child's hand; then reverse the original template and make two templates from it (so the thumb is pointing in the opposite direction) for a total of four templates.

2. Place the freezer-paper templates, shiny side down, on the wrong side of the back of your sweater, aligning the bottom of the mitten templates with the bottom of the sweater. Leave at least ½" between each template. Press the freezer-paper templates into place for 15 to 20 seconds with a dry iron set to the manufacturer's suggested temperature for your sweater. ⑦

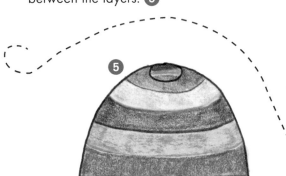

Whipstitch folded brim
to *outside* of hat.

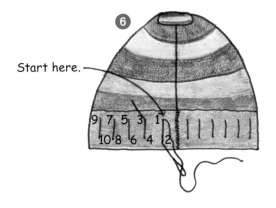

Start here.

9 7 5 3 1
10 8 6 4 2

RETIP *to match
or not to match*

If you cut your mittens as shown in the diagram, the stripes will match in each mitten, and your two mittens will match. This is optional. If you cut your shapes without regard to the print or stripe in your sweater, each mitten will be unique.

Sweater back

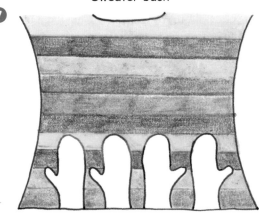

3. Cut around the four templates adding a ¼" seam allowance all around, except along the bottom of the mittens. **8**

4. Place two mitten shapes right sides together and align the edges; pin. Using a straight stitch and closely following the template edge, sew around the mitten from one side of the bottom cuff to the other. Leave the bottom cuff open. Follow up with a zigzag stitch just outside your straight-stitch seam to prevent unraveling. **9**

5. Repeat step 4 with the other two mitten shapes. Remove the freezer paper.

6. Turn one mitten right side out. Fold the mitten cuff about 1" up toward the right side of the mitten; press. Pin the pressed edge to the right side of the mitten and hand sew using a whipstitch (page 140).

7. Thread the matching or coordinating yarn onto your large-eye needle. Stitch around the mitten cuff as in "Happy Hat" step 8 (on the facing page). **10**

HAPPY SCARF

1. From the sweater remnants, cut eight 3½" x 8" rectangles. Sew four rectangles together along the short ends, first using a straight stitch and a ¼" seam allowance, followed by a zigzag stitch just outside of the previous stitches. Repeat with remaining four rectangles. **11**

Note: If you're running short on sweater fabric, cut the sleeves open along the seam and cut rectangles from the sleeve tops. Another option is to cut rectangles that are a little shorter than the original measurement (for instance, you could cut eight 3½" x 7" rectangles). You could even cut some rectangles longer and some shorter for a different look—just be sure to cut the rectangles in pairs and sew them in order so the pairs match up on both sides of the scarf.

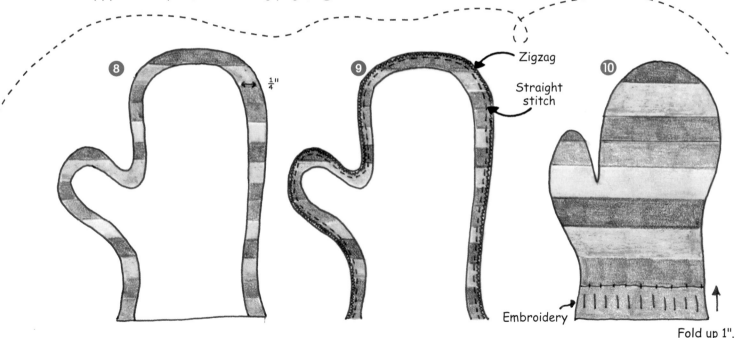

Zigzag

Straight stitch

Embroidery

Fold up 1".

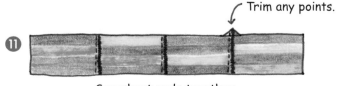

Trim any points.

Sew short ends together.
Make 2.

2. With right sides together, lay the two scarf units together on a flat surface. Pin through the layers, matching up and pinning on both sides of each seam. Sew around the scarf, starting on one short end about 1" from the corner using a straight stitch and a ¼" seam allowance. Backstitch at each end and leave a 2" opening on the short side for turning the scarf right side out. Sew around the scarf again using a zigzag stitch just outside of the previous stitching. **12**

3. Turn the scarf right side out. Use a long, blunt tool (such as the bottom of a pen or pencil) to push the corners into points. Lay the scarf on a flat surface and roll the seams outward and inward—with your fingers, as if you're using a rolling pin—until all seams lie flat. Press with an iron following the sweater manufacturer's instructions. Turn the ends

of the 2" opening inside the scarf by ¼"; pin. Hand sew the 2" opening closed using a whipstitch (page 140).

4. Thread matching or coordinating yarn onto your large-eye needle. Starting ½" in from one corner of the scarf, poke the needle in between the scarf layers. Come up through the front layer, about ¼" inside the zigzag stitch (1). Pull the knot so it's buried between the layers. Now insert the needle through ¼" from the edge of the back of the scarf (2). Keep your needle between the layers and bring it out through the front of the scarf again, about ½" from where your first stitch began (3). Insert the needle from the back (4) and repeat around the bottom of the scarf, keeping the stitches aligned. When you meet your first stitch, knot the yarn and bury it between the scarf layers. **13**

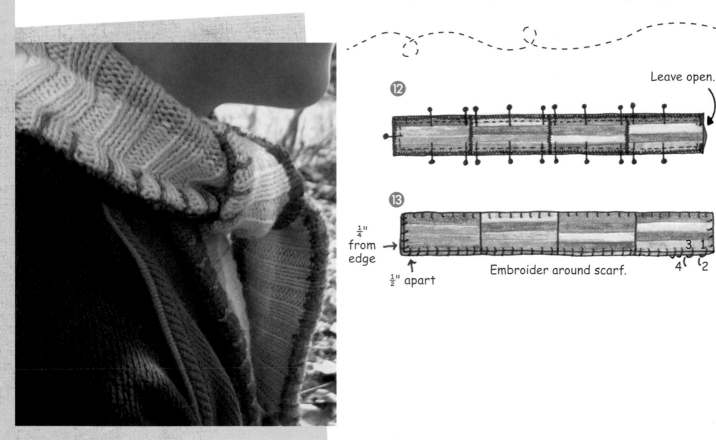

12 Leave open.

13 ¼" from edge → ½" apart   Embroider around scarf.   3 1 4 2

four-patch Sheet Quilt

If you've never made a quilt before, welcome! Although some quilt techniques can be quite intricate, this particular pattern is just about as simple as it gets. And if you are a beginner to quilting *and* sewing, watch out! For many, it only takes one quilt to become addicted for life. Proceed with caution.

It took me two months of thrifting one to two times a week to find the right colors and patterns of sheets to make this quilt. If you see just one sheet you'd like to start a quilt with, take it home. Over time, you can build on that color and/or pattern with subsequent thrift-store visits.

Finished quilt size: 48" x 64"

my fiber facts

Size: 66" x 96"/twin size

Content: 100% cotton

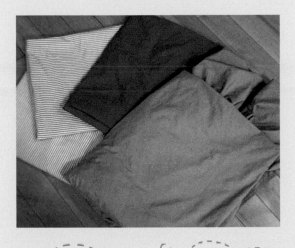

design diversions

- Instead of striped sheets, try sheets with overall patterns
- For a floral quilt, choose two sheets with large floral patterns and two sheets with tiny floral patterns
- If you have lots of sheet fabric left after cutting, consider enlarging your quilt by making more units: make 12 more of each unit to add one horizontal row; make 16 more of each unit to add one vertical row

GATHER YOUR MATERIALS

The standard size of a twin sheet is 66" x 96". These project directions assume a sheet width of at least 60" after hems and selvages are removed. If your sheets are not 60" wide, you may need to cut additional strips.

- Four 100% cotton twin-size flat sheets, two striped and two solid, in coordinating colors
- 50" x 66" piece of quilt batting
- Thread
- Rotary-cutting equipment
- Long pins
- Washable glue stick
- Masking tape
- Hand sewing needle
- Quilting hoop (optional; for hand quilting)
- Scissors (optional; for hand quilting)
- Walking foot and binder clips (optional; for machine quilting)

MAKE THE FOUR-PATCH UNITS

Note: You do not have to backstitch at the beginning and end of a line of stitching when sewing units or blocks, as the seams will be crossed and secured by other seams.

Designed and sewn by Jenny Wilding Cardon; machine quilted by Cheryl Brown

1. Cut away the seams and any selvages on all sides of one striped sheet. Cut four 2½"-wide strips from the *width* of the sheet; then cut four 2½"-wide strips from the *length* of the sheet. Repeat with the other striped sheet. **1**

2. You should have eight strips that have a short vertical stripe; we'll call these the A strips. You'll also have eight strips that have a long horizontal stripe; we'll call these the B strips. **2**

3. Pair each A strip with a B strip from the opposite sheet for a total of 8 pairs. With right sides together and using a ¼" seam allowance, sew the long edges of the strips together to make what quilters call a strip set. Press seam allowances toward the A strips (short vertical stripes). **3**

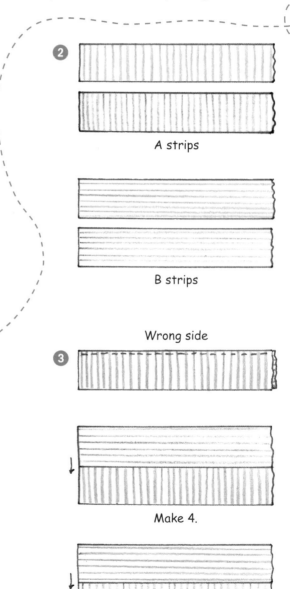

1

60"

Cut 4

2½"

Cut 4.

2½"

4. Straighten one short edge of a strip set, if needed. Crosscut the strip set into 2½"-wide units. Repeat for all strip sets. You should be able to get 24 units from each strip set, or 96 of each combination, for a grand total of 192 units. Keep the units separated into two different groups. ④

Note: Be sure to sew each pair of units on the same side every time, particularly if you're using stripes. If you don't, you'll end up with four-patch units that look exactly like the units in the other group. Take extra care with this step by laying out all of your unit pairs right sides together before sewing.

RETIP *need more?*

If you come up with fewer than 24 units per strip set, you'll need to make two additional strip sets as you did in step 1. You can cut shorter strips, depending on how many units you need. Just be sure to cut the same number of units from each strip set. For instance, if you need four more units, cut two units from the strip set with the short vertical *blue* stripe; then cut two units from the strip set with the short vertical *green* stripe.

RETIP *perfect piecing*

To get your seams to match up in the center of your units, do not pin through the seam; that will distort the stitches. Instead, bump the seams up against each other and pin on either side of the seam.

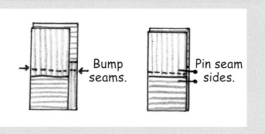

5. Pair the units from one group right sides together with the opposite fabrics touching as shown. Pin and sew the units together to make a four-patch unit. Repeat this step to sew the other group of units into four-patch units. Keep the two types of four-patch units separated. ⑤

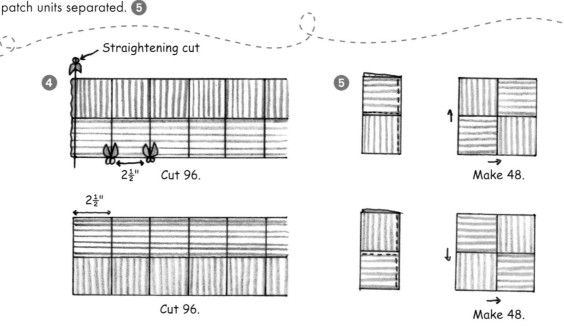

Straightening cut

④ 2½" Cut 96.

2½" Cut 96.

⑤ Make 48.

Make 48.

MAKE THE SQUARE-IN-A-SQUARE UNITS

Note: To reserve fabric for an unpieced backing, cut a 50" x 66" rectangle from one of the solid sheets before you continue cutting the strips and squares for the blocks.

1. Cut away the seams and any selvages on all sides of the solid-colored sheets. From the *width* of one solid-colored sheet, cut four 4½"-wide strips. Make a straightening cut on one end; then crosscut the strips into a total of 48 squares, 4½" x 4½". Repeat to cut 48 squares, 4½" x 4½", from the other solid-colored sheet. **6**

2. From the remaining *length* of one striped sheet, cut two 2½"-wide strips; crosscut the strips into 48 squares, 2½" x 2½". Repeat with the other striped sheet. **7**

3. Dot the back of a 2½" striped square with glue stick and finger-press it onto the center of a solid-colored 4½" square in the opposite color. Repeat this step to make 48 units; then repeat this step again to make 48 units in the opposite colors. Sew around each 2½" square ¼" from the edges, backstitching at the beginning and end. **8**

ASSEMBLE AND FINISH THE QUILT TOP

1. Follow the diagram to lay out eight four-patch and eight square units in four rows of four units each. You'll need four of each different unit to make one large block. Pay special attention to the direction of the stripes. Sew the units into rows and sew the rows together. Press seam allowances in opposite directions from row to row. Make 12 blocks. Alternate the pressing direction of seam allowances from block to block to allow seams to bump together when you join the blocks. **9**

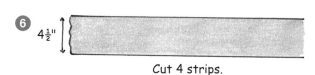

6 4½"

Cut 4 strips.

4½"

Cut 48 squares.

7 2½"

Cut 2 strips.

2½"

Cut 48 squares.

Make 48. Make 48.

Make 12.

2. Arrange the large blocks into four horizontal rows of three blocks each. Make sure that the seam allowances alternate for easy matching and sewing. Pin and sew the blocks into horizontal rows; then sew the rows together. Press the seam allowances in the direction indicated by arrows in the illustration. ⑩

MAKE A QUILT SANDWICH AND QUILT YOUR TOP

1. Make a quilt "sandwich" by layering the backing, batting, and quilt top. Place the 50" x 66" backing fabric, right side down, on a flat surface. (If you did not cut and reserve a piece of solid fabric for the backing, sew pieces together from any of your leftover sheets to get the correct size.) Use masking tape to pull the backing taut and secure it to the surface. Center the batting on top of the backing and smooth out any wrinkles. Center the quilt top on top of the batting, right side up, and smooth out any wrinkles. Secure the quilt top to the surface with masking tape as well.

2. To thread baste the layers together, start in the center of the quilt. Take 2" vertical stitches, 2" apart, up the center of the quilt, and then down to the bottom. Repeat to baste a horizontal row of stitches along the center of the quilt. Now, stitch horizontal rows 4" to 6" apart along the length of the quilt top. Repeat to baste the vertical rows. Remove the masking tape. ⑪

3. Determine the quilting pattern you want to use on your quilt. A few simple ideas for quilting this design are shown. ⑫

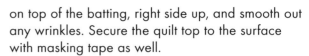

⑩
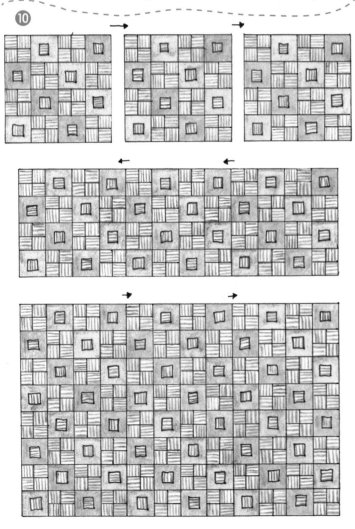

⑪
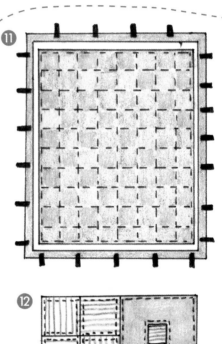

⑫
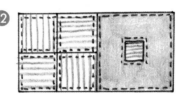

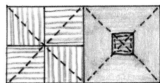

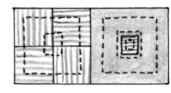
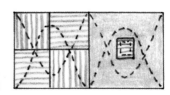

4. Mark the quilting design on the quilt top if desired. To hand quilt, you'll need a quilting hoop to hold the layers taut. Take small, evenly spaced stitches through all three layers. Instead of taking one stitch at a time, you can "load" three or four stitches on your needle at a time. Place one hand underneath your quilt at all times to make sure you are catching all the layers of the quilt with each stitch. Bury thread knots between the backing and quilt top at the beginning and end of each length of thread by gently pulling knots into the batting. **13**

To machine quilt, use a walking foot, if you have one, for straight-line quilting. Roll and clip your quilt with binder clips as you stitch each section of the quilt to help manage and maneuver the bulky layers as you sew.

5. After your quilting is complete, cut the backing and batting layers even with the size of the quilt top.

BIND YOUR QUILT

1. Lay your quilt on a flat surface. From the sheet fabric that you want to use for binding, cut the longest 2"-wide strip that you can. Lay it down around the outside of the quilt. Continue cutting and laying down strips around the edges of the quilt, overlapping the ends by 2", until your quilt is surrounded by strips, plus an extra 10". For a quilt the same size as mine, you will need about 236" of binding. **14**

2. With right sides together, overlap the short ends of two binding strips at a right angle and sew across the diagonal as shown. Trim ¼" from the stitching line; press the seam allowances open. Repeat until all strips are joined. **15**

13

End of thread   Beginning of thread

Quilt top

Batting

Backing

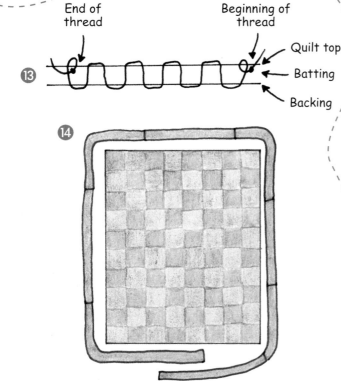

Lay binding strips around quilt edges.

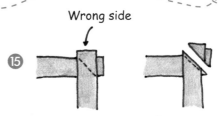

Wrong side

Sew, cut, and press.

3. Starting at one end of the binding strip, fold one corner to create a triangle, wrong sides together, and press; then press the strip in half lengthwise, wrong sides together. **16**

4. Align the raw edges of the binding (starting with the pointed corner) with the quilt top along the bottom of the quilt near the middle. Starting at the pointed end, sew using a ¼" seam allowance just until you reach the fold in the binding; end with the needle in the up position. Lift your presser foot and reposition the work slightly so that the needle can re-enter the fabric ¼" beyond the fold. Lower the presser foot and continue stitching until you are ¼" from the edge of the quilt. Backstitch and remove the quilt from your machine. **17**

5. Flip the binding up to create a 45° angle with the corner of the quilt. Fold the binding back down onto itself, even with the edge of the next side. Start stitching again at the corner. Repeat this process at each corner until you have sewn all the way around the quilt, almost to the start of the binding. **18**

6. To join the end of the binding to the beginning binding, lay the end piece along the start of the binding and cut away the excess binding where the ¼" seam starts after the fold. Tuck the end of the binding into the fold; sew until you have reached the first stitching and backstitch. **19**

7. Fold the binding over to the back of the quilt and blindstitch (page 140) the binding in place. A miter will form at each corner; add a couple of stitches to the miters on the front and back as shown. **20**

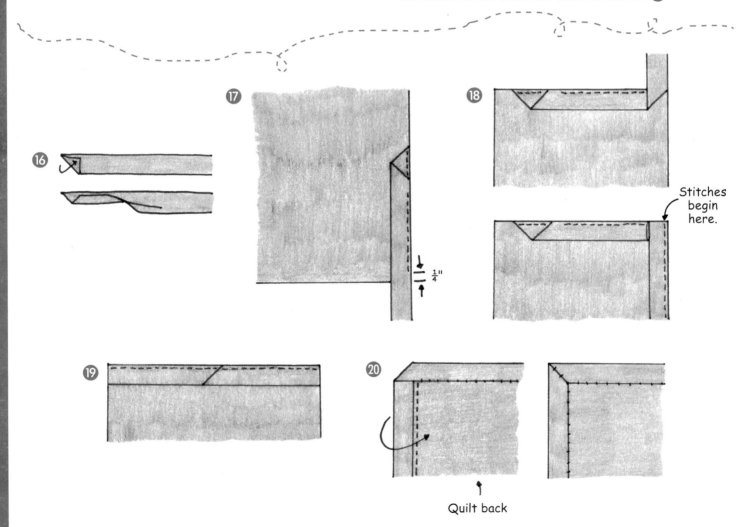

Stitches begin here.

Quilt back

paper clip RUG

This design is based on the "toothbrush" rug—a style of rug that looks very similar to a braided or crocheted rug but requires much less fabric. Toothbrush rugs, named because of the tool used to make them, were popular in the 1930s when supplies were sparse and the make-do mentality was at a peak. These wonderfully imperfect, beautifully textured rugs are usually worked in the round, but I chose to work the technique row by row. After some experimentation, I found that a large paper clip is really all you need to make every knot and loop in this rug.

It's hard to say exactly how many pairs of jeans you will need. It depends on how big you make your rug, how big your jeans are, and how tight your loops are. I suggest starting with at least three pairs (I ended up using close to four pairs). You can easily add more denim to the mix later without compromising the design.

Finished rug size: 17" x 34" (without fringe)

my fiber facts

Size: Men's 38" waist; Men's 40" waist; Men's 40" waist

Content: 100% cotton

design diversions

- Make a perfectly square rug
- Try longer fringe, thicker fringe, or no fringe
- Randomly vary the colors of your strips for a more rustic look
- Use other thrifted fabric, such as draperies in decorator-weight fabric

GATHER YOUR MATERIALS

- 3 or 4 pairs of denim jeans—the bigger, the better—in varying light and dark shades
- Thread to match denim (optional, for blind stitch)
- Scissors
- Seam ripper
- Rotary-cutting equipment (optional, but recommended)
- Safety pin
- Large paper clip (a small one will do, but a large one makes it easier)
- Hand sewing needle (optional, for blind stitch)
- Crochet hook, size J (10) or larger (for fringe)

CUT STRIPS FROM DENIM

1. With scissors, cut up the inner and outer sides of each pant leg. Cut across the waistband, along any pockets, and down the front opening; cut just below the waistband and down the center back seam. Cut away the bottom hem and carefully remove

back pockets with a seam ripper. The goal is to keep as much denim as possible in one piece, while removing all seams. **1**

2. Using a rotary cutter, mat, and ruler or scissors, cut 1"-wide strips from the length of each pant-leg piece. Long strips are best, but keep those shorter strips—they'll come in handy too. Anything at least 6" long can be saved for fringe. **2**

Note: Rotary-cutting equipment makes this project run along much quicker than scissors alone. However, scissors are definitely okay to use. If you do end up using scissors, remember that these strips do not have to be perfectly cut. Close enough will work just fine here.

MAKE THE FIRST ROW OF YOUR RUG

1. Divide your denim strips into two piles by color. Choose a color for the short edge of your rug and take two strips from that pile. Fold over a short edge of both strips about ½". Using scissors, cut a ¼" vertical slit through both layers at the fold. Repeat this for the other end and with each new strip you add to the rug. **3**

Note: Cut vertical slits as you go, rather than cutting all slits in advance. If you choose to make fringe for your rug, you'll want the strips to be uncut.

2. Align the short edges of the two strips. Make a loop with both strips aligned; pull the short edges through the loop and tighten. Safety pin the knot to a flat surface, such as a blanket on top of a bed or a carpet on the floor. This will be the first row of your rug. **4**

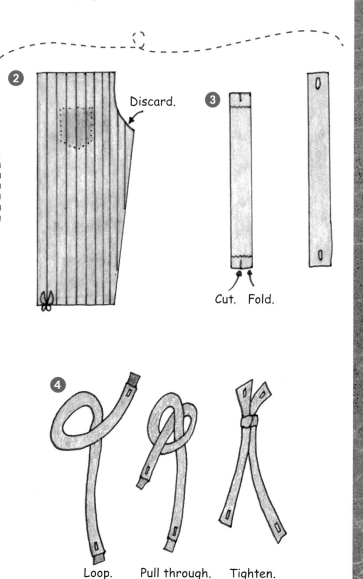

Discard.

Cut. Fold.

Loop. Pull through. Tighten.

3. Move one strip to the left and one to the right. Slide your paper clip onto the vertical slit at the bottom of the left strip so the strip is caught inside the loop of the paper clip. Make a 4 shape with the two strips, folding the left strip over the right strip to make the two short, angled lines of the 4; the right strip becomes the long, vertical line of the 4. Bring the paper clip under the right strip and through the center of the 4 shape to form a knot. Slide the knot up the right strip so it bumps into the first knot; pull it taut, but not tight (you'll need to slide your paper clip and strip through this knot later). ⑤

4. Repeat step 3 to make more knots along the first row of your rug. You can make as few or as many knots as you wish, but this first row will determine how wide your rug will be. I made 24 knots, including the first knot that ties the two strips together.

Adding New Strips

Eventually, you will need to add new strips. You may use up a strip in the first row, depending on the number of knots and the length of your strips. The left strip used for knotting will need replenishing more often than the right strip, which acts a foundation. Work until you have between 2" and 4" remaining on the existing strip, and then add a new strip.

1. Remove the paper clip if you're adding to the left strip. Cut vertical slits into both short edges of the new strip. Push one short edge of the new strip through the vertical slit in the existing strip; pull the new strip 2" to 3" through the slit. ⑥

2. Insert the longer end of the new strip through the slit in the shorter end, creating a loop. Pull the strip until it is almost knotted onto itself. Then cinch the knot tightly onto the existing strip. Reattach the paper clip to the bottom end of the new left strip. ⑦

Note: To start a new stripe or color of denim, cut the existing strip 2" to 4" from the rug. Then follow the steps for "Adding New Strips" above to knot a new color of denim onto an existing strip. After tying a few knots, your row will change to the new color.

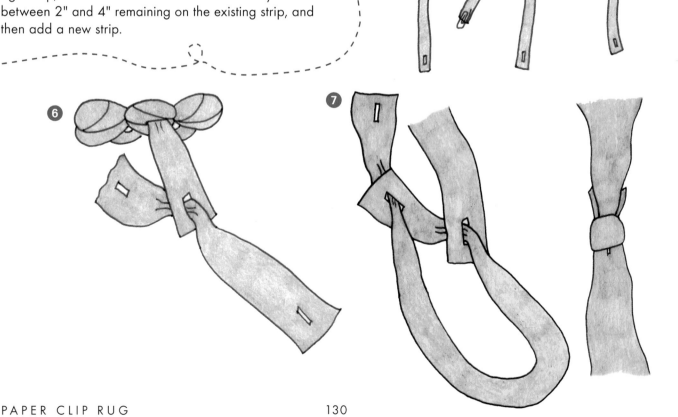

ADD THE SECOND AND SUBSEQUENT ROWS

1. When you've made the last knot on the first row, move your *body* to the opposite side of the rug so the loose strips are now at the top of your work area. Remove the safety pin from the bottom of the rug and repin it at the top. **8**

2. Place the right strip (the strip without the paper clip) *under* the left strip; then pull the right strip tightly against the previous row. Now you'll make knots as you did on the first row, but with one extra step. Make your 4 shape with the strips; then insert the paper clip down through the small hole that was created from the previous knot you made. You will do this for all subsequent rows. Bring the paper clip under the right strip and through the center of the 4 shape as before. Slide the knot up the right strip to make the first knot in the row; pull it taut, but not tight (you'll need to slide your paper clip and strip through this knot later) **9**

3. For the third row, work the knots exactly as you did in the second row *except* that you will form your strips into a *backward* 4 shape to make your knots. Going forward, every other row will require a backward 4 shape. **10**

4. Continue working each row until your rug is the length you want (my rug ended up with 52 rows). The last row should be worked exactly the same as the rows you've been working. When you reach the end of the last row, you can either use the paper clip to weave in the ends of the strips on the back of the rug or you can cut the strip ends 2" to 3" in length, turn them to the back of the rug, and fold in and blind stitch (page 140) the short edges.

Note: When starting a new row, sometimes it can be a little confusing to choose which hole to pull the left strip through. Be sure to locate the hole closest to the top of the row before making the first knot, and pay attention to how many knots you make per row; they should count out the same from row to row. If you skip a knot here and there, your rug will begin to

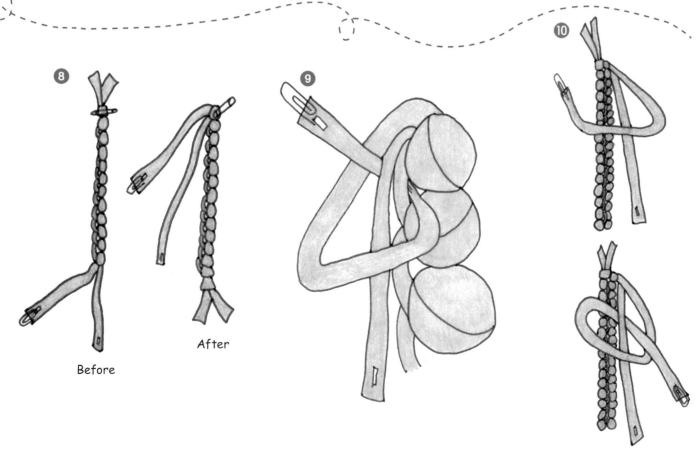

Before

After

"shrink" widthwise. If one of your rows has already "shrunk," you can easily widen it again by making a knot through a hole on the outside edge of the rug (not a hole in a row). This will give you an extra knot if you've lost one along the way, and it's close to undetectable in the finished rug.

RETIP *pinned down*

You won't need to keep the rug attached with a safety pin to something while you work the entire project, but I do suggest keeping it in play until you've worked at least four or five rows. By then the rug will have some weight and won't move around as much, and you'll have gotten the hang of how the rug handles as you make each knot.

MAKE THE FRINGE

1. Cut leftover strips into 6" pieces; then cut them into ¼"-wide strips lengthwise. (A rotary cutter, ruler, and mat are great for this.) Pair two strips together, aligning the short edges. Fold in half lengthwise. Starting on the back of the rug, push a crochet hook through a knot on one corner of the rug and come up to the front of the rug. Hook the center of the fringe strips on the crochet hook; then pull the fringe through the knot about halfway. ⑪

2. Use the crochet hook to pull the ends of the fringe strips through the fringe loop. Pull tightly toward the outside edge of the rug to secure the fringe in place. ⑫

RETIP *cut as you go*

Cut fringe one strip at a time, rather than all at once. It's difficult to determine exactly how many pieces you'll need, and you don't want to waste time cutting ¼"-wide strips that you won't use.

FINISH THE EDGES OF YOUR RUG

If you look closely at the project photo (page 128), you will see that I looped the long edges of my rug with denim strips to give it a slightly more finished look. If you love your rug as is, great—you're done! If you want to loop the long edges too, follow these steps. The process is very much like whipstitching the edges with a strip of fabric.

1. Cut a vertical slit into one short side of a denim strip. Load your paper clip onto the strip; feed the paper clip through a knot on one corner edge of the rug, from the back of the rug to the front. Pull the strip through until about 2" remain. Fold the 2" strip tail toward the center of the rug. Find the knot next to the first knot you pulled your paper clip through; feed your paper clip through the next knot, catching the 2" tail inside of the loop you create. Add additional strips using vertical slits just as you did when making the rug. ⑬

2. When you loop through the last knot on the other end of the rug, cut the strip to 2" to 3" in length and finish it in one of two ways. You can take the strip to the back of the rug and blindstitch (page 140) the short edge to secure it. Or you can use the paper clip to weave in the end of the strip on the back of the rug.

3. Repeat steps 1 and 2 to finish the other edge of the rug in the same way.

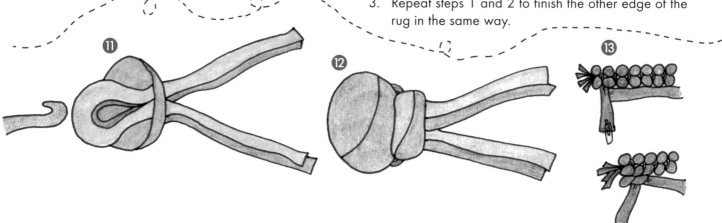

elephant cuddle CUSHION

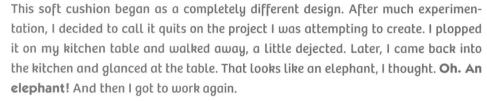
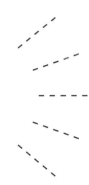

This soft cushion began as a completely different design. After much experimentation, I decided to call it quits on the project I was attempting to create. I plopped it on my kitchen table and walked away, a little dejected. Later, I came back into the kitchen and glanced at the table. That looks like an elephant, I thought. **Oh. An elephant!** And then I got to work again.

The sweater you choose needs to have some stretch—100% wool would probably not be the best choice. My sweater was completely ribbed and very stretchy indeed. The stretch is great for making a nice, big, round elephant head. And who doesn't want that?

my fiber facts

Size: Women's Large

Content: 100% cotton

design diversions

- Omit the trunk and appliqué a nose and mouth to make a silly creature cushion
- Leave the gathered edges free and eliminate buttons and trunk for a wrapped candy cushion
- Cut a smaller rectangle and sew running stitches along the edges to make a soft, stuffed ball for babies and toddlers

GATHER YOUR MATERIALS

- One women's large-size long-sleeved sweater
- Thread to match your sweater
- Acrylic* yarn to coordinate with sweater
- Two large buttons and matching thread, perle cotton, or acrylic* yarn (for eyes)**
- Five 12"-long pipe cleaners and two twist ties (for trunk)
- Pillow stuffing for head, approximately 16 ounces
- Fabric-marking tool
- Long ruler or straight edge
- Long pins
- Scissors
- Rotary-cutting equipment (optional)
- Fray Check (optional)
- Wooden spoon (for turning corners and stuffing)
- Large-eye needle (for yarn)
- Hand sewing needle
- Safety pins

*Avoid natural-fiber yarns as they break easily when pulled tightly.

**To make the elephant safe for babies or toddlers, omit the buttons and embroider the eyes with yarn.

CUT, SEW, AND STUFF
THE ELEPHANT HEAD

1. Turn the sweater inside out and lay it flat with the front on top. Use a fabric-marking tool and a long ruler or straight edge to draw the largest rectangle you can on the front of the sweater, from the bottom to the neck opening. Draw the sides of the rectangle at least ½" from the side seams. Pin around the rectangle about 1" inside the drawn lines, through both layers. **1**

2. Using a short straight stitch, sew along your marked lines through both layers. Start at the center of the bottom hem, continue up the side, around the top, and down the other side of the rectangle. Sew along the other side of the bottom hem, stopping to leave a 3" opening. Backstitch at the beginning and end of the seam. Cut out the rectangle using scissors, adding a ¼" seam allowance on three sides. **2**

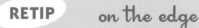

RETIP *on the edge*

Depending on your sweater's fiber content, you may want to dot a little Fray Check on the edges of the sweater along the 3" opening to prevent unraveling. In a pinch, I use a light dotting of washable glue stick to keep the yarn in place while I turn the sweater right side out and stuff it.

3. Turn the rectangle right side out, gently pushing and pulling the fabric through the 3" opening. Lay the rectangle flat and use the handle end of a wooden spoon to push the seams and corners flat.

4. Measure about 4½" in from the short side of the rectangle that does *not* have the opening for turning. Draw a dotted line parallel to the side on the front and back of the rectangle. Thread the large-eye needle with a long, doubled length of yarn. Make a large knot at the end. Insert the needle from the inside of the rectangle to the outside ¼" from one side seam and pull through at the marked line. Sew a running stitch along the dotted line through one layer only, going in and out with your needle every ½". **3**

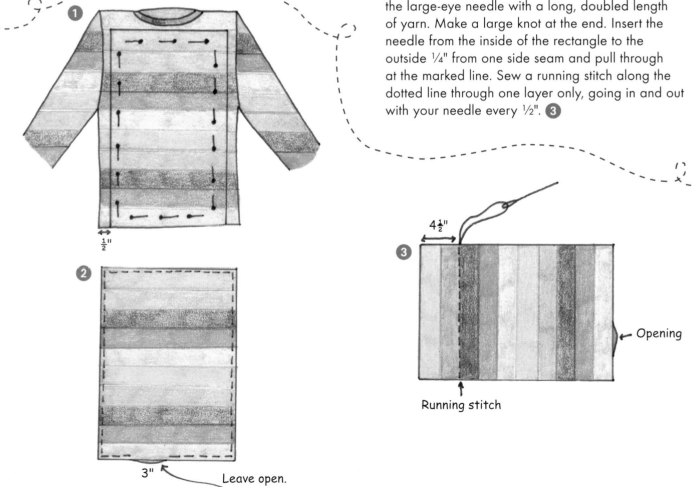

ELEPHANT CUDDLE CUSHION

5. When you reach the side seam where you started, pull the yarn to the inside of the rectangle and pull the yarn tight to cinch the sweater fabric into the elephant-ear shape. (If you pull tightly, you should be unable to see the yarn on the outside of the rectangle.) Tie a big knot inside the rectangle and cut the yarn. **4**

6. Repeat step 4 to sew a running stitch on the other side of the rectangle; however, do not cinch the yarn tight yet. Leave the threaded needle in place. **5**

7. Stuff fist-sized bunches of pillow stuffing into the head through the opening and pack with a wooden spoon until the head is big and round. Don't stretch the sweater fabric out of shape; just watch for it to look full. Cinch the second ear closed to check your progress; if you need to stuff more, just loosen the yarn stitches again. Once the head is completely stuffed, pull the yarn tightly, tie a big knot inside the rectangle, and cut the yarn. **6**

8. To sew the opening of the rectangle closed, turn each raw edge toward the inside of the rectangle ¼" and pin, or simply pinch together with your fingers a little at a time. Thread a needle with a double length of thread and hand sew across the opening with a whipstitch (page 140), catching just a few sweater fibers on each side of the seam. Refer to "Sewing Sweaters: Hand Sewing" (page 142) for tips.

9. With a doubled length of thread on a sewing needle, take a few stitches to tack the top and bottom corners of each ear to the head. **7**

ADD THE TRUNK AND EYES

1. Measure 12" from the bottom cuff of one sweater sleeve and mark a line parallel to the cuff. Cut on the marked line through both layers. Cut one pipe cleaner to 11" in length; then cut the rest to match. Gather the pipe cleaners tightly together and secure the top and bottom of the bundle with a twist tie. Place the pipe cleaners along the seamed long edge of the sleeve. **8**

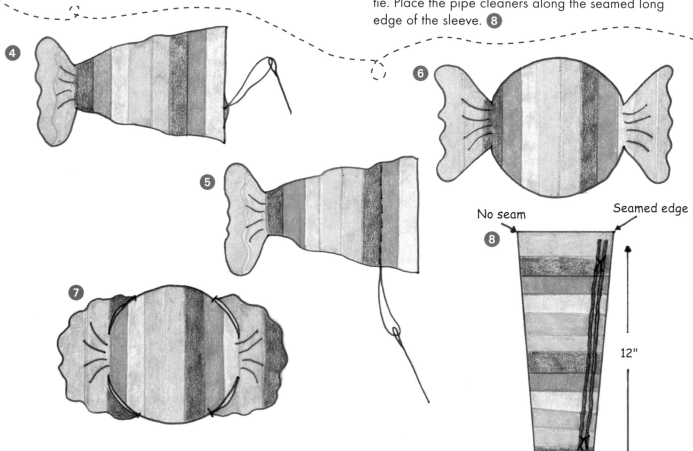

No seam   Seamed edge

12"

2. Roll the pipe cleaners *very tightly* inside the sleeve. Start at the sleeve cuff and use your fingers to tuck the sweater fabric under the pipe cleaners; continue moving and tucking your way up to the top of the sleeve. When the sleeve cuff side is entirely rolled up, pin. Keep working your way up the sleeve and pinning until the entire sleeve is rolled. Cut away any fabric sticking out of the top of the sleeve so the top of the trunk is flat and even. Using a doubled length of thread and a sewing needle, hand sew the pinned seam with a whipstitch (page 140). **9**

3. Tuck the raw edges at the top of the trunk inside the trunk a generous ¼". Follow the fabric spiral inward to tuck the fabric layers in toward the center. If the pipe cleaners are showing, bend and tuck the tips inside the trunk.

4. Thread the large-eye needle with a doubled length of yarn. Knot the yarn and take a few stitches through the center top of the trunk to secure the yarn to the trunk. Determine where you want to place the trunk on the cushion, and take a large stitch through the cushion at that point. Pull the trunk tight to the cushion; then take a few more stitches in the same place. This will ensure a strong connection between the trunk and the cushion. **10**

5. Using safety pins, pin the outer edges of the trunk to the cushion to hold it in place for sewing. Still using the same doubled length of yarn, take whipstitches that catch two or three strands of yarn from the trunk and then two or three strands of yarn from the cushion. Whipstitch all the way around the trunk, making stitches about ¼" apart. When you reach the starting point, whipstitch around the trunk once more, taking additional whipstitches between your first round of stitches. Knot the yarn and bury it inside the cushion. **11**

6. Determine where you would like to place the button eyes on the cushion. Sew the buttons to the cushion using yarn, perle cotton, or thread that matches the buttons. Bury beginning and end knots inside the cushion.

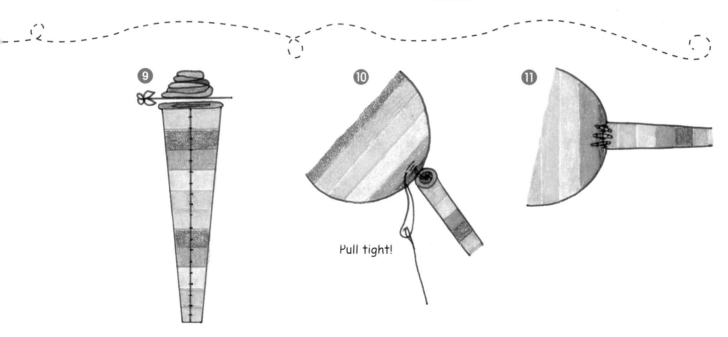

Pull tight!

I'm a sewing defector of sorts. I appreciate, respect, and rely on established rules but allow a lot of room for personal creativity between the stitches. I've followed sewing rules where they are essential and provided my own bits of what I call "renegade sewing" here and there throughout the project directions. There's a time to follow the rules and a time to bend them. (I bend them when I want what I'm working on to be done, already!) From using spice-jar lids and cereal boxes to masking tape and dinner plates for sewing assistance, I hope you'll find my more eccentric tips helpful—or at least entertaining.

If you're seasoned at sewing but new to thrifting, you may want to focus on "At the Thrift Store" (page 10) and just glance through "Back to Basics," particularly for information on working with sweaters. If you've reached professional thrift-shopper status but are new to sewing, you'll want to take a thorough look at this section. (And send me your best thrifting tips by email!)

If you're new to both thrifting *and* sewing . . . well, you've been missing out! I'm thrilled you've picked up this book. This section will teach you some sewing basics that are important for making the projects in this book.

RETIP *save those care tags!*

To avoid any doubt about how to care for or wash your resewn projects, be sure to save the care tags that came with the original thrifted items. Sew a tag into your newly remade garment or accessory and you'll never have to wonder how to wash it.

MUST-KNOW MACHINE STITCHES

The most important thing to remember about machine sewing? BACKSTITCH. Always backstitch at the beginning and end of every seam, unless otherwise indicated in a pattern. I'll even remind you to backstitch if it's super important. You don't want your hard work at the machine to come undone after a wash or two. So get in the habit of backstitching every time.

Let's go over a few standard machine stitches you'll need to be familiar with when making projects in *ReSew*.

Straight stitch. The straight stitch is the simplest and quickest way to sew one piece of fabric to another. It's used for seams, for topstitching (sewing a line of stitches on top of a piece of fabric), and for stay stitching (sewing a line of stitches near the edge of a piece of fabric to prevent stretching). Unless the instructions state otherwise, use a straight stitch to sew all the projects in this book.

You can sew a straight stitch on any fabric, although its staying power will vary. Straight stitches are most successful on woven fabrics (fabrics that don't stretch on the straight grain). You can make your stitches short and tight, for extra strength, or long and loose, for tasks like basting and gathering. Use your sewing-machine owner's manual to learn how to shorten or lengthen stitches on your machine; then test out your stitches on a piece of scrap fabric. **1**

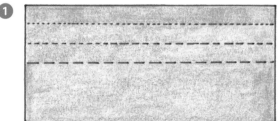

Short
Medium
Long

Experiment with straight stitches
on your machine.

Zigzag stitch. The zigzag stitch is most often used to finish the raw edges of fabric to prevent fraying. A zigzag stitch essentially encloses a raw fabric edge, lessening the ability of the fabric to fray. **2**

Using a zigzag stitch in tandem with a straight stitch is a great way to get a clean, crisp seam and prevent future fraying. After sewing a straight seam, sew a zigzag stitch so that the right side of the stitch hits just outside of the fabric edges, enclosing the fabric inside the threads.

Another option for lessening fray on fabric edges is to use pinking shears to cut a zigzag pattern.

Stretch stitch. Most newer sewing machines have the option of turning any stitch into a "stretch" stitch. When you set your machine to stretch stitch, it simply pulls and pushes the fabric back and forth as it stitches, which adds elasticity to the final seam.

When sewing a stretch stitch, let your machine do the walking. Don't be tempted to pull or push the fabric; just gently guide the fabric under the presser foot so the stitches are sewn where you want them.

I recommend a stretch stitch for stretchy fabrics, such as T-shirt fabrics, sweatshirt fabrics, and sweaters (unless they're made from wool). If your machine doesn't have a stretch stitch option, try a zigzag stitch, which can also increase the elasticity of a seam.

Overlock stitch. An advanced version of a zigzag stitch, the overlock stitch is present on almost every article of commercially manufactured clothing you own. It does a great job of enclosing raw edges and sewing a clean seam to show off on the outside of a piece. Many standard sewing machines now have an overlock stitch option. **3**

Although I have an overlock machine (also called a serger), I decided not to use it for the projects for this book. I wanted anyone with a basic sewing machine to be able to make every project in the book. If you do have an overlock machine, however, I encourage you to substitute overlock stitches for zigzag stitches and to overlock any raw edges you think may fray over time.

Many overlock machines also have the ability to sew stretch stitches. But that's another book!

MUST-KNOW HAND STITCHES

Over the past dozen years—most of them as a quilter—I have fallen in love with hand sewing. It takes time. It takes concentration. It takes skill. Did I mention it takes time? Perhaps that is what I love most about hand sewing—the time it takes. The process can instantly slow you down and bring you to a "be-here-now" moment. And we all need that sometimes.

I don't have a huge catalog of stitches in my head; I have just a few that I rely on for just about any task.

Running stitch. The running stitch is the most basic stitch in hand sewing. It's used to sew basic seams and hold fabric layers together. Simply push the needle down through the fabric and back up again, and then pull the thread through. You can make several stitches with the needle before pulling the thread all the way through. The goal is to make all of the stitches equal in length. **4**

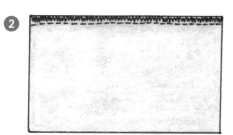

A zigzag stitch combined with a straight stitch

Example of an overlock stitch

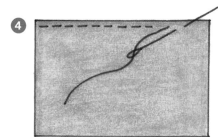

Running stitch

Whipstitch. You can use this versatile stitch for many purposes: to hand sew openings closed, hold two layers of fabric together, or finish raw edges of fabric. You basically push the needle through one layer and out the other—"whipping" the thread around the folded or raw edges. Make whipstitches close together for added strength. ❺

Blind stitch. The blind stitch (or appliqué stitch) is very close in technique to the whipstitch except for the "blind" part—if it's done properly, you really can't see it! Use this stitch when you're attaching one fabric on top of another, such as for appliqué or binding. Push your needle through the background fabric from behind; pull the thread taut. Catch just a few threads from the edge of the top fabric, push your needle back down through the background fabric, and pull the thread taut. Repeat, keeping stitches close together for strength. ❻

MUST-HAVE SUPPLIES

Every seamstress—budding or pro—needs a stash of tried-and-true supplies. These are the basic tools I rely on whenever I sit down to sew. If you're just starting a supply stash, designate a large basket or bag as your sewing-supply catchall and you'll have your tools at the ready whenever you want to sew.

Rotary-cutting equipment. I've been quilting for over a dozen years, and that's how I was introduced to the rotary cutter, cutting mat, and acrylic rotary-cutting rulers. These tools are all but essential to quiltmaking. They have also made all kinds of sewing easier, quicker, and more precise for me. I've had the same rotary mat and rotary cutter for at least seven years (although I have replaced the blade on my rotary cutter several times). I have quite an extensive collection of rotary rulers—square, rectangle, long, short, huge, tiny. If you plan to sew on a regular basis, they're an investment you won't be sorry you made. I suggest starting with an 18" x 26" rotary cutting mat, a 12½"-square rotary ruler, and a 45 mm rotary cutter. You will never want for more! (Except more rulers, maybe.)

Needles. I must admit, I don't usually know the size number of any hand sewing needle I happen to be using—my favorite needles simply have eyes that I can get my thread or yarn through! There are oodles of numbered needle sizes out there. But for me, there are just two types of needles I always have around—common hand-sewing needles for sewing with thread and yarn needles (also called darning or tapestry needles) for sewing with yarn. You can get sets of both in assorted sizes at your local fabric store for less than $5 to start. From there, you can experiment with the sizes you like best.

Measuring tools. In my mind there are three types of measuring tools that enable me to measure just about anything: dressmaker's measuring tape, a rotary ruler, and a common school ruler. Dressmaker's measuring tape is pliable, so it will measure around curvy things (like your hips and your bust). A rotary ruler will quickly measure (and with a rotary mat and ruler, will easily help you cut) straight edges, squares, rectangles, triangles, and strips. A common school ruler is great for any quick measuring you need to do—I keep mine close

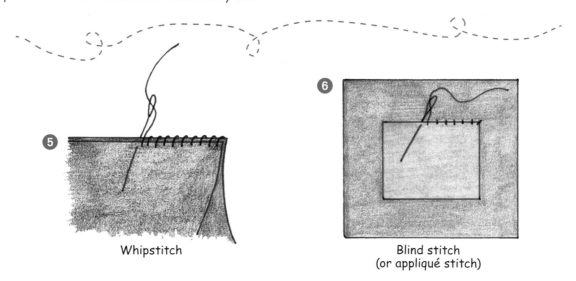

Whipstitch

❻

Blind stitch
(or appliqué stitch)

by my sewing area at all times. (And I do believe it's my original school ruler, from like, umpteen years ago.)

In a measuring pinch? Try yarn. Thread. A necklace. A belt. Licorice. Whatever. If you gotta measure, you gotta measure.

Straight edges. I have accumulated a pile of acrylic rulers that could rival my local fabric store's shelves. From teeny-tiny to wide and square to long and skinny, I've found that the right size acrylic ruler—otherwise known as a rotary ruler—can turn a difficult cutting task into a no-sweat situation. But sometimes, I'm working upstairs and all of my rotary rulers are downstairs. And when you're sewing, you want to *get on with it* already! So I always have a common school ruler on hand (both upstairs *and* downstairs). For drawing straight lines, I've used books, folders, square and rectangular lids, sticky notes, and my kitchen cutting board. Those are the items I can think of, although I know I've used others. If you just need to connect a line from point A to point B, a ruler is great. But just about anything else that will stay straight works, too.

Marking tools. There are a lot of fabric-marking tools to choose from—water-soluble pens, air-soluble markers, colored chalks, marking pencils, transfer pads, even glowing tape! I like air-soluble markers, but they are expensive and tend to dry out very quickly (both the marker and the marks you make). Until recently, I bought three air-soluble markers at a time and replenished them when they ran dry. Then I realized that what I really needed had been hiding in my little boys' art cabinet all along—washable markers. They are inexpensive, come with narrow or wide tips in a rainbow of colors, and last a while (as long as you keep the lids on, Jack and Charlie!). I've experimented with these markers on all kinds of fabric with great results. I suggest marking and washing a small area on the wrong side of your fabric before you begin, but time and time again I've been able to simply run a piece of fabric under cold water or throw it in the wash to get the marker out.

Pins. Whether I'm pinning clothing, quilts, accessories, or accents, I use 1¾"-long pins with yellow heads, also known as quilters' pins. They're especially helpful when you want to pin through the thick layers of a sweater. I also use safety pins for a variety of tasks. My mom gave me a box of safety pins that said "10 gross" on

the label. I didn't know what a gross was until I looked it up (it's a count of 144). Safe to say I have enough safety pins to last my lifetime.

SEWING SWEATERS

Sewing on knits may be new to you, but it's not difficult. I've tried several methods; here's what works for me.

Machine Sewing

The result of machine sewing on sweater knits will always be a little wonky. Own that characteristic as part of your one-of-a-kind design and let the texture and stretch of a sweater add interest to your work. I created the Sweater Scarves (page 90) with simple squares in mind; instead, I ended up with slightly skewed edges that I think add a personality and charm that you would never see had I achieved my original goal of perfect squares. Thank goodness for happy accidents!

When I began sewing with sweaters, I was straight stitching, stretch stitching, zigzagging, and overlocking all over the place because I was afraid the sweater fabric would unravel after cutting. The experiments were frustrating, and the results were often stiff, obliterating what people most love about sweaters—their comforting, cozy softness. When I took a step back and tried one machine stitch at a time, I found that the simplest stitch is most often the best stitch for a sweater. Now, whenever possible, I use a straight machine stitch.

Sweater fibers react to cutting and machine sewing in different ways. When a different kind of stitch is required in any of the project instructions, I let you know what worked best for me. The most important tip I can give you is to handle cut sweaters with care. Once a sweater has been cut, excessive pulling, tugging, and roughness will distort the knitted fabric at best, and unravel it at worst. Here are a couple of helpful tips:

• **Stretching.** Believe it or not, I found that, even more than a stretch stitch on my machine, a firmly knotted hand basting stitch near the edge you want to machine sew helps prevent a lot of stretch in a sweater. It simply holds the sweater in place while you sew. And a quick hand-basted seam beats unpicking machine stitches every time.

- **Unraveling.** Some sweaters are prone to unravel. When you're trying to stuff a sweater with fiberfill or attempting to turn a tube inside out, unraveling at the unsewn opening can become a problem. Try dotting the raw edges with Fray Check before you begin your task. In a pinch, I've applied dots of washable glue stick on an area I'm afraid might begin fraying, with good results.

Hand Sewing

I've also done quite a bit of hand sewing on sweaters, and I've come up with an easy and sturdy technique for knotting at the beginning and end of a hand-sewn seam. Here's my method, in three simple steps.

1. Always use doubled thread. Thread the needle; then knot the two ends together to form a loop of thread. **7**

2. To start a line of stitching, guide the needle through the sweater fabric where you want to begin. Before you pull the knot tightly against the sweater (and it pops out the other side!), draw the needle through the loop formed by the knotted end of the thread. Now pull the thread snug and hide the knot between layers or along the inside edge of the thread. The thread will be held securely in place so you can begin your line of stitching. **8**

3. To end a line of stitching, tie a large knot in an inconspicuous place; then take three to five tiny stitches over the knot and cut the thread close to the sweater fabric. **9**

FELTING WOOL SWEATERS

Felting wool sweaters is an easy technique—you wash and dry the sweater by machine—but there are a few rules to keep in mind. Let's walk through the process step by step, and I'll share some of my unexpected results.

1. Fill your washing machine with hot water and a little detergent. Add the sweater and a terry towel or two and run the machine on a normal cycle. Set the rinse cycle for cold water.

2. Stop the cycle after each agitation phase (this is the part of the washing cycle that felts the sweater) and check the size of your sweater. You want to make sure it doesn't shrink so much that you won't be able to use it for your intended purpose.

   My unexpected result for step 2? I had a sweater shrink to a toddler size so fast that I could not possibly use it for my intended purpose. Every sweater will react differently to a machine wash, so check on it often. If your sweater is felted to your satisfaction before the final rinse, remove it and rinse it by hand in the sink. Then roll it up in a towel to press out the excess water, reshape it, and lay it flat to dry.

3. Machine dry your sweater as you would a normal load of laundry, tossing in a few clean towels to help the sweater dry evenly. Easy enough.

   My unexpected result for step 3? I remember once having balls upon balls upon balls of wadded-up wool fall out of the dryer upon completion of a dry cycle. The sweater was fine; it just shed like a Saint Bernard in summer. My lint trap was of some help, but not much. Some people advise enclosing a sweater in a mesh bag or pillowcase when machine felting. I think, going forward, that will be a good plan to follow.

4. Once your sweater has gone through one complete cycle, check to see if you can still see the knitted rows in the sweater fabric. If you can, it likely needs more felting. Repeat the process. Once the stitches blend into each other, the sweater is ready for cutting and you won't have to worry about the edges unraveling.

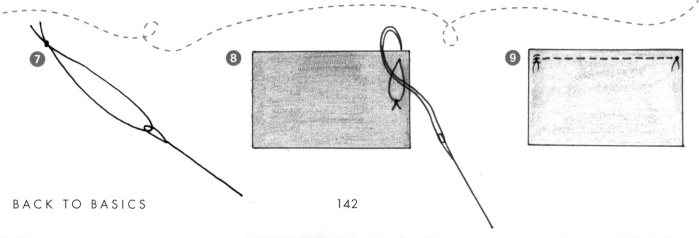